THE WINDOW OF AFFORDABILITY

A PRIMER FOR
BAY AREA FIRST-TIME
HOME BUYERS

BY STEVEN A. LYONS

First Edition

Library of Congress Catalog Card Number: 87 - 90485

Printed in the United States of America

ISBN 0-9618084-0-3

STRATOSPHERE PUBLISHING

6116 Merced Avenue
Box 211
Oakland, California 94611
(415) 486-1310

Disclaimer: Every effort has been made to ensure the accuracy of the information in this book. However, errors do occur, both typographical and informational. For legal guidance, consult an attorney. The author shall have no responsibility or liability for damages or alleged damages arising from the use of information contained herein.

Cover Design: Sandy Biagi
Window Illustration: Doug McCarthy
Text Layout: Diana Lorentz

Table of Contents

The real estate industry is constantly changing. You can help others like yourself by calling to my attention any outdated material. Also, if you have a particularly bad experience with any of the organizations listed in the reference and resource section, let me know. Finally, send any information appropriate for the reference and resource section to:

Stratosphere Publishing
6116 Merced Avenue Box 211
Oakland, CA. 94611

PART ONE

SHOULD I BUY? CAN I BUY?

Over the past half decade, the usual flow of first-time home buyers into the real estate market has slowed to a trickle, held in check by a dam of high interest rates.   However, the recent plummeting of interest rates to a ten-year low has sent a flood of first-time home buyers rushing into the housing market. In the 1980s, most renters have assumed that the American dream of home ownership is out of their reach, and have therefore remained ignorant of the complex world of real estate.   This book is a crash course on real estate, addressed to those who want to take advantage of the present window of affordability. By the end of this primer, the real estate novice will have gained insight into whether he or she should or can buy, and also begin to understand the whole morass of financing a foray into the real estate jungle.

This is a four-part book.   Part One investigates two questions: Should I buy? Can I buy? Part Two discusses house hunting and purchase offers.   Part Three examines creative home buying, and the book closes with a large reference and resource section.

SHOULD I BUY?

The first question the potential buyer must ask is not "Can I buy?" but rather "Should I buy?" There is no law that requires every human being to stop fooling around and settle down with a nice deed of trust by age 28, regardless of what your mother says.

Initially, ignore whether or not you can afford a home. To determine whether you should buy a house, ask yourself "What do I want? What are my goals? What will make me happy?" Make a list of your answers to the above questions. Objectively scrutinize your list. Would home ownership enhance your aspirations or inhibit them?

To determine if home ownership will help you down the path to your goals and dreams, carefully consider all the ramifications of owning a home. Subsequent sections revel in the delights of home owning. But let's pause for a moment to consider home ownership's negative side. What should you be considering now, to avoid disappointment in the future?

The rosy flower of home ownership has four thorns.

Before you own a home, you must buy it first. The substantial time investment to find and purchase a home is the first thorn. Reading this book is just the tip of your real estate education iceberg. After splashing about in a sea of real estate books and seminars, you then must spend innumerable weekends looking at houses and talking to realtors. Upon finding a house you're interested in, you must do exhaustive research on the home, make offers, counter offers, talk to banks and apply for loans. If you are over-committed in other areas of your life, perhaps the added burden of a housing search should be postponed.

Once you've bought the house, then its physical upkeep is your responsibility, which is the second thorn. If you have a penchant toward funky little houses, remember they usually come equipped with funky little toilets, which are your responsibility when they explode. No more calling the landlord when the roof leaks or when the cockroaches become unbearable. To maintain its health, this 20,000 cubic foot baby nurses on your money and your time. Do you want such a demanding child in your life right now?

Along with the physical upkeep of the house comes the financial upkeep of the mortgage, which is the third barb. If your after-tax monthly loan payment is substantially higher than your current monthly rent payment, carefully weigh the effect of that financial hardship on your future. So owning a house may be a bad idea if, for example, you plan to work only part time next year, or if you hope to save money to buy a boat. As will be seen, by deducting mortgage interest from your taxes, the monthly loan payment may approximate your current monthly rent payment. But if it doesn't, brace yourself for a substantial impact on your lifestyle. And even if that monthly obligation doesn't impinge on your money, it may impinge on your spontaneity. For example if you get a once-in-a-lifetime chance to spend the summer working on an Alaskan cruise ship, you may find it difficult to take advantage of the opportunity. Unlike a landlord, you can't give a lender 30-days notice.

And finally, you must endure the down payment thorn. So even if your lender is willing to accept 30 days notice, you can't go up to Alaska anyway, because all your savings for such frivolities are sunk into the down payment on the house! Similarly, the down payment money is not available for such causes as starting your own business, traveling, or medical emergencies.

Think of your relationship with this house as a marriage contract, only worse. There is no well-defined way to divorce a house.

If, after all this self reflection, it appears you should pursue real estate ownership, next determine whether you can pursue real estate ownership. Can you afford to purchase your own living space?

7

CAN I BUY?

Home Loans

The median price for a home in the Bay Area is $166,000. Few people have that amount of money sitting around, so they need to borrow it. Therefore, to determine whether you can afford to buy a home, you must understand, and even wallow in, the filthy, high-finance world of **Bank Loans.**

Before we examine a typical loan from a bank, let's ease into it with a nontypical loan, to get a feel for the concepts. Let's say you borrow $100 from the bank. The bank lets you keep the $100 for one year. But after one year you must return the full $100. While you have the bank's money, the lender requires 12% interest per year, paid in monthly installments. Since 12% of $100 is $12, you will pay the bank $1.00 per month for one year, then return the $100. This type of loan is called a "one-year, interest–only, fixed-rate loan with a balloon." The "balloon" is the repayment of the principal (the $100) at the end of the loan period.

Prior to the '40s, most loans were "balloon" type loans. Every five or ten years the principal would come due (i.e., the "balloon" had to be paid by the borrower). It is for this reason that so many homes were repossessed during the Great Depression.

With the passage of Regulation Q following World War II, mortgage money was created for prospective home buyers. Regulation Q allowed savings and loan companies to pay 1/4% higher interest than banks. This differential was substantial enough to induce most savers to deposit funds in savings and loan institutions rather than banks. However, Regulation Q stipulated that the savings and loans had to reinvest funds in home loans. Therefore, a great pool of capital flowed into the housing market. The loans made by the savings and loans differed from those made prior to World War II. These new loans were "fully amortized" loans, which means that over the life of the loan, the loan is gradually paid off. This was the distinguishing feature of this financing method.

Let's now make our $100 one-year loan similar to these post-war loans, namely "fully amortized." This gets mathematically intense. However, comprehending the concept is more important than understanding the arithmetic.

In addition to monthly interest payments, a fully amortized loan requires monthly repayment of part of the principal. ("Principal," remember, is another word for "amount borrowed.") In this way, at the end of the loan period, the loan is completely paid off—no more "balloon" payment is involved. Since part of the principal is paid to the bank every month, the balance of the money owed the bank decreases every month. Since interest is charged on the amount of money still owed the bank, the monthly interest payment decreases.

Now suppose that, even though the interest payment decreases, the monthly payment to the bank remains fixed. Stated as an equation, we have:

interest payment + principal payment =
fixed monthly payment

the money attributed to principal increases every month as the money attributed to interest decreases. Therefore, the total monthly payment remains fixed.

Figure 1 depicts how the one-year fully amortized loan of $100 evolves over the course of a year and how the loan is completely paid off in 12 equal payments.

Note from the table that the total amount paid to the bank is $106.60. In the case of the balloon-payment loan, the total paid to the bank was $112.00. The fully amortized loan, for a given loan period and a given interest rate, is usually a better deal. The only advantage of the balloon-payment loan is that the monthly payments are lower: $1.00 per month compared with $8.89 per month in this particular case.

9

Figure 1. Progression of a One-Year Fully Amortized Loan

Annual percentage rate: 12%
Original loan amount: $100.00
Monthly payment: $8.89
Term: 12 months

Payment #	Interest Payment	Principal Payment	Balance of Loan
1	$1.00	$ 7.89	$ 92.11
2	.92	7.97	84.14
3	.84	8.05	76.09
4	.76	8.13	67.96
5	.68	8.21	59.75
6	.60	8.29	51.46
7	.51	8.38	43.08
8	.43	8.46	34.62
9	.35	8.54	26.08
10	.26	8.63	17.45
11	.17	8.72	8.73
12	.08	8.73	0
	$6.60	$100.00	

A typical home loan is not $100, but closer to $100,000. A $100,000 fully amortized one-year loan at 12% interest would require monthly mortgage payments of $8,884.88. This is a little steep for most borrowers. But lenders have seen this dilemma and taken mercy upon the masses. Instead of requiring that the loan be fully amortized in one year, they have stretched the repayment period to 30 years. Since the borrower has longer to return the original amount borrowed, the monthly mortgage payments are lower.

As an example, let's examine what happens to the $100 loan if it is converted from a "one-year, fully amortized" loan to a "30-year fully amortized" loan. As the second figure shows, the monthly loan payment goes from $8.89 to $1.03. The loan payments are now nearly equivalent to the interest-only balloon-payment loan. In fact, most of the monthly payment is dedicated to interest in the early years of the loan. Note that the first payment reduces the outstanding balance by only 3 cents. Since in the initial years of a 30-year loan, your monthly payment is mostly interest, you repay the bank much more money than you originally borrowed. In the present example of $100 at 12% interest, you pay the bank $370.80 over the 30-year period, i.e., $270.80 in interest.

Figure 2. First Payment of a 30-Year Fully Amortized Loan

Annual percentage rate: 12%
Original loan amount: $100.00
Monthly payment: $1.03
Term: 30 years (= 360 months)

Payment #	Interest Payment	Principal Payment	Balance of Loan
1	$1.00	$ .03	$ 99.97

The House Affordability Equation

Now let's extend these ideas to the actual purchase of a house.

Typically, the money borrowed from the bank covers 80% of the purchase price. The rest of the money must come out of your pocket. This out-of-pocket money is called a "down payment." The down payment plus the financing equal the full price of the house.

A financial institution determines the amount of money it lends you based primarily upon your monthly income. The lender looks only tangentially at the value of the house. It's you, not the house, that makes the monthly mortgage payments. Only in foreclosure is the house value of concern to the bank. And the bank doesn't want to foreclose. Foreclosure is a pain in the neck to the bank. The lender greatly prefers a steady flow of monthly mortgage payments from the borrower. For this reason, even if you locate a fabulous deal on a house, don't expect the banker to get as excited as your best friend. The lender still demands that you meet minimum income requirements.

And what are these minimum income require-ments? Typically financial institutions require that no more than 28% of your gross monthly income be dedi-cated to PITI (principal, interest, property tax, and property insurance). Furthermore, banks demand that your monthly PITI payments, plus any other long-term debt payments, be no more than 36% of your gross monthly income. These percentage figures are known as "qualifying ratios."

The house you can afford is further influenced by the "closing cost," which is the money withheld from the loan proceeds to cover the lender's fees, the escrow fees, the title insurance premium, and local taxes. Part Two of this series examines closing costs in more de-tail.

Clearly, the house price you can afford is influ-enced by an overwhelming array of variables. Down payment, interest rate, closing cost, property tax, property insurance, your monthly income, and the lender's qualifying ratio must all be accounted for. Figure 3 presents the relation between these factors as three separate equations. By solving the equations sequentially (plugging the answer from one equation into the next equation), you can estimate the house price you can afford. Figure 3 makes some assumptions that greatly simplify the equations. First, it assumes that your monthly loan payment is all interest, no prin-cipal. Recall that this is essentially true during the initial years of a 30-year loan. Secondly, it assumes property tax plus property insurance comprise 2% of

Should I Buy? Can I Buy?

Figure 3. The Affordability Equation

Eq. 1 $M = R \times$ your monthly gross income $\times .98$

Eq. 2 $F = \dfrac{M \times 12}{I}$

Eq. 3 House price you can afford $= D + (F \times .95)$

M = Monthly loan payments you can afford, according
to the lender.

R = Ratio used by lender to qualify borrower; use
decimal equivalent (e.g., 28% = .28).

F = Amount the bank will lend you. A more precise
value of "F" can be found using a mortgage table.

I = Interest rate on loan; use decimal equivalent.

D = Down payment.

---

your monthly loan payment. This 2% translates into the
".98" coefficient of Equation 1. Closing costs are estimated at 5% of the loan amount. This is where the
".95" fudge factor in Equation 3 originates. As an example, let's determine how much house can be purchased by a family earning the Bay Area median
income.

The median family income in the Bay Area is about
$3,000 per month. Assume this typical household has
saved up $26,062 for a down payment. (This down
payment figure was carefully chosen to equal 20% of
the house price, as will be seen.) Assume the lender's
qualifying ratio is 28%, and that the interest rate on
the loan is 9%. As derived in Figure 4, the house this
typical family can afford costs $130,308. Unfortunate-
ly for our typical family, the median price for a house
in the Bay Area is $166,000, $36,000 beyond what the
average family can afford!

If you find this depressing, you are not alone. The
National Association of Realtors publishes statistics
that quantify just how depressing the housing situation
is. Called the "affordability gap," this figure measures
the difference between the monthly median income and

Figure 4. Typical Bay Area Household Affordability Calculation

R = .28
Monthly income = $3,000
I = .09
D = $26,062

Eq. 1   M = .28 x $3,000 x .98 = $823.

Eq. 2   F = $823 x $\frac{12}{.09}$ = $109,733

Eq. 3   House price family can afford
    = $26,062 + ($109,733 x .95) = $130,308

---

the monthly income needed to purchase a median-priced home. According to the figures, the last time the nation's median-family income could qualify to purchase the median-priced home was 1978. The affordability gap was worst in 1981, when the median income in the U.S. was less than two-thirds the income required to purchase a median-priced home. Presently, the nationwide annual median income of $29,000 per household is barely enough to purchase the nationwide median-priced home of $83,000.

When you plug your own salary and down payment figures into the equation, set the value of R to .28 (28% monthly loan payment to monthly income ratio) and be sure to exclude from your gross monthly income any interest presently earned on the money to be used as a down payment. To determine "I", assume a 30-year fixed-rate loan. The interest rate on such a loan can be found in the real estate section of your newspaper or obtained from your local bank.

If you discover you can barely afford the neighbor's doghouse, then Part Three is for you. Although the Bay Area housing situation is bleak, it is possible for a first-time home buyer to purchase a house. Part Three is dedicated to bridging the affordability gap.

Before leaving the affordability equation, let's examine one final detail. Equation 2 uses the simplifying assumption that the entire monthly mortgage payment (M) is allocated to interest payments. But the mortgage payment of an amortized loan covers not only interest but also principal. So the affordability equation is more accurate if we use an "amortization table" instead of Equation 2. Amortization tables list monthly mortgage payments for any given loan amount, loan period, and interest rate. They are available from the library, book store, stationery store or reference 11. Figure 5 is a section from an amortization table.

Figure 5. Amortization Table

Interest Rate	8%		9%		10%	
Loan Term	15	30	15	30	15	30
Loan Amount						
1,000	9.56	7.34	10.15	8.05	10.75	8.78
2,000	19.12	14.68	20.29	16.10	21.50	17.56
3,000	28.67	22.02	30.43	24.14	32.24	26.33
4,000	38.23	29.36	40.58	32.19	42.99	35.11
5,000	47.79	36.69	52.72	40.24	53.74	43.88
6,000	57.34	44.03	60.86	48.28	64.48	52.66
7,000	66.90	51.37	71.00	56.33	75.23	61.44
8,000	76.46	58.71	81.15	64.37	85.97	70.21
9,000	86.01	66.04	91.29	72.42	96.72	78.99
10,000	95.57	73.38	101.43	80.47	107.47	87.76
20,000	191.14	146.76	202.86	160.93	214.93	175.52
30,000	286.70	220.13	304.28	241.39	322.39	263.28
40,000	382.27	293.51	405.71	321.85	429.85	351.03
50,000	477.83	366.89	507.14	402.32	537.31	438.79
60,000	573.40	440.26	608.56	482.78	644.77	526.55
70,000	668.96	513.64	709.99	563.24	752.23	614.31
80,000	764.53	587.02	811.42	643.70	859.69	702.06
90,000	860.10	660.40	912.84	724.17	967.15	789.82
100,000	955.66	733.77	1014.27	804.63	1074.61	877.58

Should I Buy? Can I Buy?

Using Figure 5 instead of Equation 2, we discover the median-income family can qualify for a loan of $102,000, which is indeed close to the $109,733 given by Equation 2 of Figure 4. The details of using the amortization table are shown in Figure 6.

Figure 6. Using the Amortization Table

A monthly payment of:	Yields a loan amount of:
$804.63	$100,000
+16.10	+2,000
$820.73	$102,000

The family can afford a monthly loan payment of $823. They are considering a 30-year fully amortized loan at 9% interest. If Figure 5 had a listing close to $823, the loan amount could be read directly from the table. Since it does not, this two-step process is required.

Tax Implications

The lender doesn't consider your potential tax savings when determining whether you can afford a home loan. On the loan application you state your gross income (i.e., before tax), so your tax situation is not accounted for. However, when you are deciding whether you feel you can afford a house, your tax situation most assuredly should be considered. The interest paid on your home loan may be deducted from your income, thereby reducing your income tax. Therefore, your home may be a fantastic tax shelter as well as a physical shelter. Deduction of interest paid on the mortgage of a principal residence is one of the few tax write-offs left untouched by the recent tax overhaul.

Let's take an example and see how tax saving works. This analysis accounts for the new tax laws.

Figure 7. Tax Rate Schedule

<u>1987</u>
Single

Below 2,540	$ 0					
$2,541-$4,340	0	+	11%	of amt. over	$2,541	
$4,341-$19,340	198	+	15%	"	"	4,341
$19,341-29,540	2,448	+	28%	"	"	19,341
$29,541-56,540	5,304	+	35%	"	"	29,541
Above $56,541	14,754	+	38.5%	"	"	56,541

Married

Below $3,760	$ 0					
$3,761-6,760	0	+	11%	"	"	$3,761
$6,761-31,760	330	+	15%	"	"	6,761
$31,761-48,760	4,080	+	28%	"	"	31,761
$48,761-93,760	8,840	+	35%	"	"	48,761
Above $93,761	24,590	+	38.5%	"	"	93,761

<u>1988</u>
Single

Below $3,000	$ 0					
$3,001-20,850	0	+	15%	"	"	$3,001
Above $20,851	2,677	+	28%	"	"	20,851

Married

Below $5,000	$ 0					
$5,001-34,750	0	+	15%	"	"	$5,001
Above $34,751	4,462	+	28%	"	"	34,751

Personal Exemption
1987	$1,900
1988	$1,950

The new tax schedule and personal exemption rates for 1987 and 1988 are shown in Figure 7.

17

Should I Buy? Can I Buy?

Batya makes $30,000 per year, and in 1987 paid $10,000 on a home loan. For simplicity, assume the $10,000 is all interest. Remember in actuality it's part interest payment and part principal payment. The principal is not tax deductible. After she takes the $1,900 personal exemption, her taxable income is $28,100. Without interest deductions, she would pay $4,900 in federal income tax. However, if she deducts real estate taxes and the home loan interest payments from her income, her tax liability becomes $2,028. The tax savings is therefore $2,872 or about 29% of the $10,000. Figure 8 details the calculations.

Figure 8. 1987 Federal Income Tax

	Without Deduction	With Deduction of Mortgage Payments	Difference
Income	$30,000	$30,000	
Personal Exemption	1,900	1,900	
Property Tax	0	1,560	
Mortgage Payment	0	10,000	
Taxable income	28,100	$16,540	
Tax	$ 4,900	$ 2,028	$ 2,872

When a more rigorous analysis is done which includes state tax savings, the mortgage payment is found to be reduced by 37%! The tax considerations effectively reduce a monthly house payment of $833 to $528. You can see why there is a public outcry any time Congress attempts to dismantle this tax-saving legislation.

Should I Buy? Can I Buy?

For a rough estimate of tax savings, simply look up your income tax bracket in the "Tax Rate Schedule" from Figure 7. For example, in Batya's case, a single taxpayer in 1987 earning $30,000 annually is in the 35% tax bracket. This is fairly close to the 37% found upon detailed analysis.

Rent Versus Own

These tax benefits, in conjunction with other considerations, make home ownership less costly than it would appear initially. For example, Batya may shudder at the thought of an $833 per month mortgage payment. However, an "after-tax" mortgage payment of $528 per month may approximate what she would have paid in rent. Were Batya to base her "rent versus own" decision entirely upon financial considerations, however, she must take into account much more than tax differences. Housing appreciation, closing costs, rental inflation, home-loan interest rates, Realtor's commission, utilities, tax rate changes, savings-account interest rates, maintenance costs, property tax, and insurance premiums must all be considered in comparing the cost of renting a home to the cost of buying a home. But the question, "Does it pay to own?" is important enough that we should roll up our sleeves and tackle it. By making certain assumptions we can greatly simplify our task.

We will compare Batya's housing costs for five years. In one case she rents for five years and invests the money she would have used for the down payment and the closing costs. In the other case she uses her savings as a down payment on a house, lives in the house for five years, and then sells.

Let's investigate owning first, and base our analysis on the following assumptions: The house costs $120,000. Batya divides her $25,000 savings between the closing costs ($5,000) and the down payment ($20,000). She obtains a 30-year fixed-rate loan of

Should I Buy? Can I Buy?

$100,000 to cover the remainder of the house price. The mortgage payments are about $10,000 per year (thus our tax analysis done earlier holds true.) Assume that the housing costs outlined in Figure 9 rise with inflation at an annual rate of 5%. Batya's mortgage payments remain fixed over the five-year period. Batya's income increases at the rate of inflation. The tax schedule also follows this 5% inflation rate, and therefore her tax bracket doesn't change over the five years. The interest she may deduct from her income tax decreases slightly every year. For simplicity, we assume it remains fixed at $10,000 per year. The average annual housing appreciation in the Bay Area over the past ten years has been about 10%, and that figure is used in our analysis.

Figure 9. Housing Costs in Addition to Mortgage Payments

Property Tax	Hazard Insurance	Maintenance & repair	Utilities	PMI
1.3%	.5%	1.5%	1.0%	.4%

Costs expressed as a percentage of house price. All these except PMI (private mortgage insurance) will rise with inflation over the years. PMI is discussed in Part 3.

Figure 10 details the calculations. After living in her home for five years and then selling, her profit is $21,316. The income tax liability Batya will encounter upon selling the home has been ignored, because she may defer the tax by purchasing another residence within 24 months.

If she rents, the $25,000 she used for the down payment and closing costs could be invested at 10%

Figure 10. Housing Cost

	At end of First Year	Total after Five Years	Summary
Own			
House price: $120,000			
Initial loan: $100,000			
Closing Cost: $5,000			
Credits			
House value	$129,600	$193,261	
Tax savings	2,872	14,360	
			+207,621
Debits			
Loan balance	99,400	96,200	
Loan payments	10,000	50,000	
Property tax	1,560	8,619	
Property insurance	600	3,314	
Maintenance & repair	1,800	9,945	
Utilities	1,200	6,631	
			-174,709
Realtor's commission			-11,596
Owner's total gain			+21,316
Rent			
Initial rent: $600/mo.			
Investment: $25,000			
Credits			
Investment balance	26,625	34,250	+34,250
Debits			
Annual rent payments	7,200	39,816	-39,816
Renter's total gain			-5,566

interest. She is taxed on this extra income. Therefore, to make the comparison accurate, we assume she withdraws part of the interest every year to pay the extra income tax the interest creates. The effective interest is therefore 6.5%. It is estimated that a $120,000 home could be rented for $600 per month. Her rental cost is therefore $7,200 the first year, and increases by 5% every year. Her account after five years minus her rental costs results in a negative cash flow of $5,566 over the five-year period. So the total difference between home ownership and renting is $26,882 in favor of home ownership. Put another way, home ownership saved her about $5,380 every year.

So should Batya buy a house or rent? Based on the assumptions outlined above, the figures suggest she should buy. But if we alter any one of the assumptions upon which this analysis is based, the answer to the above question may change dramatically. Many of these assumptions are based on predictions of the future, which is usually difficult to do (and predicting housing appreciation is nearly impossible.)

I must emphasize that renting a home, instead of buying, is not the worst financial catastrophy in the world. If upon finishing this book, you determine renting is your only option, it doesn't mean you are doomed for economic disaster. In the present economy of moderate interest rates, moderate appreciation, and steep home prices, **home ownership is not a financial panacea**. However, there are ethereal benefits to owning that defy economic analysis. What is it worth to be able to dig up the yard and plant a garden, or put nail holes in the wall, or add a darkroom? Upon settling into my own home, I found a sense of roots, of belong-ing, that had eluded me during my many years as a renter. Furthermore, I began to open my home to friends and relatives in a way I had never done as a renter, probably because I had never felt it was my home to open.

If the economic analysis in Batya's case indicated renting and owning were financially comparable, I would advise her to buy a home. Since the figures in fact suggest that she may be $27,000 ahead if she buys, I would strongly urge her to go for it!

PART TWO

HOUSE HUNTING AND PURCHASE OFFERS

This section examines the nuts and bolts of house hunting and purchase offers. Searching for a house, as one might expect, is both fun and nerve wracking. By being prepared and keeping a few principles in mind, one can accentuate the former and reduce the latter.

DO YOUR HOMEWORK!

I cannot overemphasize the importance of arming yourself with real estate basics before jumping into the trenches. Luckily this is not difficult to do, and plenty of resources are available to help you through real estate boot camp. For example, the real estate section of your local newspaper is bursting with valuable information. Just how valuable varies from one newspaper to another. Figure 11 rates several San Francisco Bay Area papers. Go to the library and read real estate sections from the past three months. While you're there, check the back issues of <u>California Real Estate</u> magazine. Locate other magazine articles on real

Figure 11. San Francisco Bay Area Newspapers

	Real Estate Section		Mortgage Table	
	Day	Quality[1]	Day/ Section	Source[2]
Times (Contra Costa)	Sunday	Poor	Sun./R.E.	R/N
Chron./Exam. (San Francisco)	Sunday	Great	Sun./R.E. Mon./Bus.	R/N (3)
Mercury News (San Jose)	Sat.	Good	Mon./Bus.	R/N
Tribune (East Bay)	Sunday	Poor	Mon./Bus.	R/N
Times Tribune (Peninsula)	Sat.	Good	Sat./R.E.	R/N
Bee (Sacramento)	Sat./Sun.	Good	Sun./R.E.	R/N
Union (Sacramento)	Sat.	Good	Sat./R.E.	(4)

Notes:

(1) Poor: mostly press releases, no real estate columnists.

Good: informative articles, some columnists.

Great: informative articles, many columnists, seminar announcements, etc.

(2) R/N: Real/Net. The rates listed in the newspapers are a sampling from their Bay Area survey, and do not necessarily represent the best offerings from the survey. A lender that services a limited area is listed only in the newspaper serving that area. See reference 76.

(3) The Chronicle business section surveys the same lenders every week.

(4) Rotates the lenders in survey every week.

estate, housing finance, house buying, and mortgages by looking up these headings in the library's "Index of Periodicals." Having done this, check out a book on real estate. Inundate yourself! You have not done enough research until Fannie Mae and Paul Volker are haunting your dreams!

In conjunction with this reading, the serious buyer may also consider taking a short course or seminar on real estate. Seminars are listed in the real estate section of the paper. The resource section at the end of this book also lists many educational sources on real estate.

Having mastered the basic concepts, it is time to confront the most terrifying question of your life. With "Ride of the Valkyrie" blaring on the stereo, look in a mirror and ask yourself, "What sort of house do I want?" You save yourself tremendous frustration and time by knowing what you want before hitting the streets.

To determine what you want, begin by choosing a house-hunting price range. You have already solved the affordability equation assuming 30-year fixed-rate financing. This is the lower end of your price range. Now return to Figure 3 and plug in an interest rate 2% lower than the fixed-rate loan. This gives your upper price limit.

Continuing your sojourn of self-reflection, determine the features you want in a living environment. Luckily, there is a marvelous book to assist you on this leg of the journey. Designed to be written in and referred to like a workbook, A House Hunter's Diary (reference 8) is the What Color Is Your Parachute? of real estate. It includes an excellent section on determining the type of house you want to buy and the type of neighborhood you want to live in. Having decided on the features you want in a living environment, establish priorities by dividing the features into three categories: "must have," "should have," and "would like to have." Shoot for a house that includes most of your "would like to have" characteristics, and don't bother looking at homes that don't meet your "must have" criteria. Give this stage of your homework careful consideration. Nothing is more distressing than buying a house, only to realize one year later that it wasn't really what you wanted!

REAL ESTATE AGENTS

To get your feet wet, grab the Saturday or Sunday real estate section of the paper and look for "Sunday Open House" advertisements. Drive around, see what's out there. Meet your very first, real live real estate agent. Go to some snazzy areas. Try the complimentary white wine and brie. Have fun!!!

Most open houses have flyers available that list details of the layout of the house, lot size, seller's name, age of house, present financing, seller's asking price, and so forth. If there is a real estate agent involved, engage him or her in conversation. Read the flyer and ask questions about anything you have trouble understanding.

Real estate agents are a special breed of human, and you should approach them fully aware of their strengths and weaknesses. Unfortunately, realtors can be dangerous. They are tampering with extremely serious items--namely vast sums of your money and your time. For most people, the purchase of a house is the largest financial commitment they make in their life. Most (but not all) real estate agents lack both the training and the mind set to give a home purchase the educated scrutiny and serious attention it deserves.

When dealing with real estate agents, remember this simple fact: they are not there to help you, they are there to sell you something. If you want help, you're going to have to get it yourself.

Only when you feel confident with your own knowledge should you approach a real estate agent. It is not imperative that a realtor be used in executing a home purchase. However, in your housing search you are sure to encounter them. A good real estate agent can be a real blessing and a vital component to a successful home search. Just be certain that, in the end, you rely on your own knowledge and judgment.

Realtors are licensed by the state upon successful completion of a few classes in real estate. They make their living from commissions on property they sell. These commissions, which are paid by the sellers, are typically 6 or 7% of the sales price. The same house being sold without a real estate agent may be lower in price by 6 or 7%, or the seller may ask the same price and simply pocket the extra money.

A seller lists a property with a real estate agent for two reasons. The first is to take advantage of the training and experience of the agent. This training and experience will hopefully result in a better sales presentation and in a well-prepared sales agreement. The second reason is that by listing with a real estate agent, the seller's property is described in a "multiple listing" book. This book, which is a weekly service of the Board of Realtors, outlines all properties for sale by all the real estate agents in the area. If the client of another agent buys the property, the listing agent and the buyer's agent split the sales commission.

A buyer goes to a real estate agent for similar reasons: the agent's training and experience, and the agent's access to information on an enormous number of houses via the multiple listing service. To a buyer, this multiple listing book is extremely handy. It carries photos of the houses for sale in the area, along with pertinent information on sales price, financing, house size, and so on. The multiple listing book also documents the actual selling price of local houses. This is helpful in determining true property values (as opposed to asking prices). The multiple listing service does not list "for-sale-by-owner" houses.

Unlike the arrangement between the seller and the seller's agent, there is no formal agreement between a buyer and an agent. A buyer may use many realtors in a housing search. However, since all agents in any given area have access to the same multiple listing service, there is little advantage in working with more than one agent. And in fact, if you work exclusively with one agent, the agent is likely to be much more dedicated and willing to invest time and energy to your search.

And how do you find an agent, if you want one? You encounter many agents simply by attending open houses and calling upon homes advertised in the paper. If, in so doing, you discover an agent with whom you feel comfortable, tell that realtor you would like to work exclusively with him or her.

In one multiple listing area I found an agent with whom I hit it off immediately. She had a funky car (which actually died while we were out in the country, forcing us to hitch-hike back to town). She was able to accept the fact that I was on a budget. Many agents tried to talk me into something more expensive, saying my budget was not realistic. I agreed to work exclusively with her. If I saw a house advertised in the paper, I would not call the listing agent directly. I would call my agent and she in turn would phone the listing agent. If a sale eventually evolved, she would get half the commission. And in exchange for always including her in any potential sale, she dedicated a lot of time and energy to my housing search.

Remember that if an agent shows you a house, the seller is obligated under contract not to sell to you directly but only through that agent. Some contracts are written so that even after the listing expires (one to three months), the seller is still forbidden to sell to you directly if the house was originally shown to you by an agent.

Some people are hesitant to buy a house without involving an agent, so they steer clear of "for-sale-by-owner" homes. However, if the contract and financing are simple, and you have done enough study and research, you should be able to write the sales contract yourself. If the deal is complicated, then a real estate attorney will probably be required to help with the contract anyway, with or without a real estate agent. So, provided you have done your homework, you should have no problem executing a sales agreement without a realtor, if you need to.

Under contract, both your agent and the seller's agent work for the seller, because they are both paid by the seller. As of January 1988, realtors in California will be required by law to disclose to buyers in writing just who they actually represent. The three representation alternatives are "sub-agency," "dual-agency," and "buyer's agency." If your agent represents you in making an offer on a home listed by another broker, then your agent is a sub-agent and exclusively represents the interests of the seller. If your agent represents you in making an offer on his or her own listing, then your agent is a dual-agent and represents all parties equally. However, from a practical standpoint, the agent is paid by the seller and therefore the agent's allegiance is to the seller.

If you have done your homework, and approach your agent fully aware that anything you say will reach the ears of the seller, then it does not matter that the agent actually represents the interests of the seller because you are not relying on your agent to do your thinking for you. However, if you feel more comfortable with a broker who is acting exclusively in your best interest, you may consider retaining a "buyer's agent." These realtors perform all the normal services, but without the conflict of interest. The loyalty of a buyer's agent lies with the buyer because they are paid by the buyer. The three primary avenues of paying for their services are: (1) an hourly fee, (2) a flat fee based on the amount of money you expect to spend, or (3) a percentage of the house cost. In the last case, the buyer's broker and seller's broker might each get 3% all paid at closing, so there is no increase in the total cost. (For further information, see references 66, 67, and 68.)

THE SEARCH IS ON!

There are a few tricks to ferreting out the exceptional deals when hunting for a home. The most important axiom of bargain hunting is: buy the cheapest house in a good neighborhood, never the nicest house in a bad neighborhood. Why? Because homes in a bad neighborhood, even the best homes, appreciate in value much more slowly than homes in a good neighborhood. A bad neighborhood is defined as one with a high crime rate and an undesirable school district. The glaring exception to this axiom is an "up and coming" neighborhood, where residents are actively rejuvenating their homes and environment, perhaps with the assistance of the local government's rehabilitation department.

Another bargain-hunting method is to locate a motivated seller. For example, homes listed in the paper in the middle of the week indicate a more anxious seller than those listed only on the weekend. Determine why the seller is selling. If the owner is being forced to sell because of a divorce or job change, for example, she or he is more apt to wheel and deal than if there are no precipitating circumstances.

A third bargain-hunting technique is to limit your competition. Don't go out house hunting on a picture-perfect spring day, when both birds and prices are soaring. Wait for a dismal streak of weather. With most home buyers huddled by the fireplace, you should be out splashing the pavement. Also, the papers are filled with homes for sale during November and December, but most prospective buyers are preoccupied with the holidays. A perfect time for a sneak attack. Another technique for limiting your competition is to buy the property before it is placed on the market. Part Three explores this avenue.

A low sales price is only half the bargain-hunting story. A home may have an average price tag yet carry exceptional financing, making it a bargain deal. Financing bargains are investigated in Part Three.

House Hunting and Purchase Offers

Upon locating a house you're interested in, don your Sherlock Holmes cap and prepare to sleuth. It's time to investigate the home thoroughly and determine if you really want to buy it. If other potential buyers are following close on your heels, make your purchase offer immediately, but make it contingent upon the results of your research. However, if the home won't be stolen from beneath your feet, then take the time to research the house before making a purchase offer. This way you can consider the results of your research when deciding how much to offer. To prevent unnecessary expense, postpone any inspections that cost money until after the offer is accepted.

A wealth of information on any given property resides in the crypts of your local city and county government. To begin your sleuthing, visit the city's building department and department of public works. At each department ask to see the file on the property. These files reveal everything from recent additions to the house to problems with the sewer system. While you're there, drop by the planning and zoning department to ask about flooding, erosion, streets destined for expansion, fault lines, brush fire hazards, and any planned industry or apartment complexes. Also ask about the policy on variances; if they are granted easily and often, zoning laws have little meaning.

After the check at the city, visit the school your children will attend. The school district office or local Board of Realtors can usually refer you to a school-by-school comparison of student tests. Even if you have no children, the school district plays an important role in the resale value of the home. In addition, the crime rate in the neighborhood influences both the resale value of the home and your happiness while living there. The local police department can give you crime statistics for any given area. Reference 9 thoroughly investigates San Francisco Bay Area school rankings and also outlines city-by-city crime statistics.

House Hunting and Purchase Offers

When you reach the point of making an offer on a house, you should have done enough hunting that you instinctively know the approximate value of the house. But if you need a "Bluebook" comparison, ask your realtor to show you the multiple listing's "cumulative index" for the area. This index outlines asking price, selling price, number of days on the market, and other details about recently sold homes. The price the seller paid for the home may be determined from the local transfer tax, available at the county recorder's office. Keep in mind that any loans the seller assumed are not reflected in the transfer tax. For yet further peace of mind, you may ask the seller to show you any recent appraisals of the house.

A "title report" states the legal owner of the house, as well as what bank, if any, holds the loan on the house. The title report may also list other liens and encumberances against the property. You should ask to see a copy of the title report early in the buying process. Title reports will be discussed later in greater detail.

A used car buyer wouldn't purchase a car without first taking it for a test drive. However, the same concept has yet to be accepted by the real estate industry. Although it is frowned upon by both realtors and sellers, demand that the house pass a 24-hour test drive. Treat the sellers to a night at a fancy hotel and move in for 24 hours. It is money well spent should you discover that the street doubles as a short cut for rush-hour traffic, or that the backyard doubles as an opium den for neighborhood kids. Since this costs you money, do it after your offer is accepted, by making your offer contingent upon the house passing this inspection.

While you have the house out for a test drive, you might as well open up the hood and really get your hands dirty. You can teach yourself the basics of inspecting a house by studying any of the many "how-to" house inspection books. I recommend the excellent book by George Hoffman, How to Inspect a House (reference 6).

If the lender feels it is warranted, a "termite report" may be required before a loan is issued. These reports warn of termite damage, dry rot, and other structural problems. The lender may require that repairs be made before the loan is granted. Even if the lender doesn't require a termite report, you may want to hire a professional housing inspector to confirm your own judgments of the home. Listed under "Building Inspection Services" in the Yellow Pages, a housing inspector provides a detailed written analysis on the soundness of the home. Fees are about $250. Include in your purchase offer the ultimate escape clause: "This offer contingent upon buyer's or his/her representative's complete inspection and approval of the property." This is the "cold feet" escape clause. Even if the inspection reveals few flaws in the house, it is possible to disapprove the findings, and thereby get out of a legally binding contract. If the inspection reveals problems with the house, you can continue to search elsewhere, ask the seller to make the necessary repairs, or lower your offer to compensate for the unfavorable inspection.

In addition to an inspection, a home warranty can provide further peace of mind. These one-year warranties, available from "American Home Shield" (reference 85), cover malfunctions due to normal wear and tear in wiring, plumbing, built-in appliances, water heater, and furnace. The buyer typically pays the premium of $325.

Home warranties are also available on new homes. New home warranties became more uniform in 1974 with the creation of the Home Owners Warranty (HOW) Corp. (reference 94). Under HOW, new homes are protected against cosmetic, utility, and structural defects for two years by the builder, and against structural defects for the next eight years by HOW. If during the first two years the builder either cannot or will not respond to claims by the buyer, the HOW program honors the builder's obligation. The HOW premiums are paid by the builder.

PURCHASE OFFERS AND THE LAW

There are serious legal implications to making a purchase offer on a house. The purchase offer must be carefully worded to avoid costly mistakes. Real estate purchase forms ease some of the anxiety of making serious legal errors. These forms, which are not standardized, can be obtained from the local Board of Realtors, references 11 or 13. At the top of the form you will find the words **"This is More Than a Receipt For Money. This is a Legally Binding Contract. Read It Carefully."** This phrase never failed to make my hands sweaty.

In the body of the contract the terms of the sale are spelled out. The contract outlines the down payment, the financing, and any special conditions of the sale.

If the offer is accepted by the seller, a deposit called "earnest money" is given to a title company. The amount is not set by law, but is typically less than one percent of the sales price. Since this can be a substantial sum, it is imperative to describe carefully the conditions under which the earnest money is returned. If the purchase actually transpires, the deposit is applied toward the down payment.

Contingency clauses stipulate conditions under which the contract becomes null and void and the earnest money is returned to the buyer. One common clause is the inspection contingency discussed earlier. A second common contingency involves financing. For example, the clause might read: "This offer contingent upon buyer and property qualifying for a new 30-year first mortgage of at least $30,000 with a fixed interest rate less than 10% with a loan fee not to exceed $1\frac{1}{2}$ points." If such a loan proves to be unavailable, the buyer can either accept the best available terms or get the deposit refunded.

Stipulate a "day of closing walk through" as the final contingency to be waived. This ensures that upon transfer of ownership to you, the house is in acceptable condition and any amenities that were to be included in the sale, like built-in stereo or drapes, are indeed still there.

I made eight purchase offers in my two-year search for property. In all eight cases the offers were ultimately accepted by the sellers and I backed out of every deal except one. I never once had to forfeit my deposit money, thanks to carefully worded escape clauses.

One final note on the content of these contracts. For every action to be taken by the seller or buyer, specify a reasonable time limit, such as five working days.

HAGGLING

As in purchasing a used car, negotiating is an accepted practice in home buying. A few anecdotes from my own experience will serve as examples of what to expect in the bartering process. Although the majority of my offers were for land, the concepts hold for house buying as well. Hopefully, the spirit of adventure and even playfulness will come through. It is a rare experience to wheel and deal with such large numbers. Be careful, but enjoy it!

I found a plot of land that was a house builder's dream. It was a one-acre plot that abutted 600 acres of public land, with few other houses around. The land sloped gently upward, leveling off into a field nestled amongst oak trees. And it was priced $20,000 below comparable lots in the area. I nearly died.

The realtor assured me that since there was a house right across the street, all the utilities were easily accessible. I decided to double check. Just as I suggested to you earlier, I ravaged the city and county files. I then called the gas and electric company, the sewer district, the telephone company, the sanitation company, and the water district. Everything checked out fine except at the water district. The water district representative explained that the border of the water district was defined by the road on which the land was located. Yes, the house across the street had water, and no, I couldn't have any of it. Bringing water to the property involved hooking onto the water main one mile away, at an estimated cost of $40,000. I dropped the land, and the agent, like a hot potato.

This brings up the issue of "disclosure" on the part of real estate agents and sellers. Consumer protection laws have rendered the old adage "Let the buyer beware" almost obsolete. Recent California legislation requires realty agents and sellers to disclose all known defects by completing a "Real Estate Transfer Disclosure Statement." This also applies to property sold "as is." You should request this disclosure document in "for-sale-by-owner" transactions as well. If, after purchasing the property, you discover an undisclosed defect, you must prove the realtor or seller knew about the defect to get them to pay for damages. This can be difficult. Therefore, to avoid costly mistakes, do your homework.

In the case just mentioned, my preliminary research revealed such a horrendous problem that no purchase offer was made. However, in other cases, any problem discovered in the preliminary research simply became a consideration in the amount offered.

For example, one wooded lot I found in the hills had been pre-graded for a driveway and an area had been leveled off for a foundation. A beautiful stream ran through the property, which had a view of an East Bay regional park. Once again, I nearly died. And once again, I did my research.

This time, when I inquired about the property at the department of public works, the man at the counter just laughed, and presented me with a file that was about three inches thick. In wading through the paperwork, I discovered that the grading had been done illegally, was not up to city code, and was causing the surrounding hillside to erode and slide into the houses down the hill. In addition, the beautiful stream would have to be diverted through a cement pipe before a house could be built. I decided to pursue the lot anyway, making my offer contingent upon inspection by a soils and foundation engineer. In the purchase offer, which was far below the asking price, I stated I was aware of these various city code violations. This statement was included more for its psychological impact than its legal implications.

My offer was rejected. A counter offer was made by the seller, with a three-day time limit on my acceptance or rejection of the counter. I felt the price they were asking in the counter offer was too high, and I immediately rejected it. However, I instructed my real estate agent to not inform the sellers or their agent of my decision. I wanted the three-day time limit to expire, and then have them come to us.

On the third day, indeed, the seller's realtor called my agent. My agent casually explained that the seller's counter was unacceptable and that his client was looking at other properties. The first part was true, the second part wasn't. I really wanted that lot.

The ploy got the desired result. Within the hour the seller's agent had called back three times and the sellers had called twice. They said I should make a new offer. Now things were getting fun. I made a new offer, only slightly different from my first offer. Since I was starting to feel cavalier, I included the statement, "This is the buyer's final offer. No counter offer will be considered." The sellers accepted immediately. The engineer's report was very unfavorable, so I eventually backed out of the deal.

The property I ultimately purchased went through several iterations of offers and counter offers. The land was on the market for $60,000. From county records I determined that the seller had paid very little for the lot only a few years back. The lot was "for-sale-by-owner" and the owner was not actively advertising it. Therefore, my negotiating tactic was based on using time to my advantage.

I presented my offer of $45,000, including $5,000 down. The seller countered with $50,000, including $20,000 down. I said that was impossible and stopped pursuing it, at least in the seller's eyes.

I then played a waiting game. I somehow knew this was the land for me. Furthermore, I had been looking at property constantly for two years and was growing weary. However, I wanted to create the appearance of being disinterested, in the hope that the seller would feel some regret that the sale had been lost, and would therefore become more willing to accept my terms. Every day that passed I wanted to phone the seller with a new offer. I was afraid someone else might buy the land. Also, I wasn't really confident my ploy would work. But I waited, for two months.

I increased my offer to $50,000, with $10,000 down. Incidently, I decreased the interest rate of the note to the seller, so the total money paid to the seller was equal to my original offer—it just looked like more money on paper. The seller accepted immediately. Whether waiting had actually had an impact on the attitude of the seller, I'll never know. But the end result was what I wanted.

Notice there is a common thread running through all these anecdotes. In every case I did thorough research. Not only did this research yield more favorable purchase agreements, but occasionally prevented disastrous mistakes. And in every case I didn't get caught up in the heat of offers and counter offers, which, believe me, can become exhilarating. My attitude would have been strikingly different had these been highly desirable properties with potential buyers clambering over me to get at them. But regardless of how desirable a house appears, never, ever fail to do exhaustive research. Appearances can deceive.

AFTER THE PURCHASE OFFER . . .

When an offer is made, the deposit is held in "escrow" by a "title" company. Let's examine these terms more closely.

Remember as a kid how your brother would grab one of your Lincoln Logs and not give it back? After a few times you learned the solution to the problem was to grab his bag of marbles and hold it hostage. After sufficient screaming, crying and physical abuse, you both would say, "OK, let the baby have his toy." But, of course, you didn't simply return the items in question. There was always the possibility the brat would grab his marbles and ditch you and never return your Lincoln Log.

The solution to the problem was to render arbitration to an impartial third party—Mom. You would each hand the ransomed items to Mom and she would execute the exchange. And she was happy to do it. Why? Because she knew it was preparing you for what you would encounter later in life, escrow.

Escrow is a system in which an impartial third party acts as agent for both seller and buyer, or for both borrower and lender. The third party carries out instructions, delivers papers and documents, and disburses funds. For this service the escrow company charges a fee of around $200, although it varies with the purchase price.

Now, returning to the sibling rivalry, let's say you steal your brother's bag of marbles, yet it doesn't have the desired effect. Your brother doesn't seem to care and confiscates your entire Legos collection to demonstrate his animosity. You later discover the reason for his defiant attitude. The marbles indeed do not belong to your brother, but are borrowed from his best friend. Had you known then what you're about to learn now, you would have demanded a title search be done before pillaging your brother's stash.

Title is the record of all parties holding a lien or easement on the house. A house held as collateral for a loan is said to have a "lien" against it. An "easement" is recorded against the house if another party must enter upon the property from time to time. For example, a neighbor may need to cross the property to get to his home, or a utility company may need to enter the property to access a public utility. All of this is recorded on a title report, which is provided by a title insurance company. The title company may also act as the escrow agent. Not only does the company provide the report, but it also guarantees the accuracy of the report with "title insurance." For example, if after the purchase the IRS attempts to foreclose on you to satisfy a $10,000 federal income tax lien against the seller, the title insurance company will settle the claim. The one-time insurance premium costs $300 to $500, depending on the home price. Never buy property without obtaining a title report and title insurance.

The most common type of title insurance is a lender's policy, which insures the mortgage lender against losses due to title defects. An American Land Title Association (ALTA) policy is another name for a lender's policy. In addition to an ALTA policy, insist on an "owner's policy" to guard your own equity against losses rising from title disputes. Most buyers aren't told of this second policy.

Incidently, examine the title carefully. Since this is an important legal document one would think the title company would go to great pains to make it immaculate. However, upon studying the one I was issued before purchase, I discovered my name was spelled wrong, the wrong county was specified, and the lot numbers were incorrect.

I have alluded to a "deed of trust" without fully explaining what it is. Back to the sibling dispute. Your mom finally gets wise and sends your creepy brother to summer camp. He asks to borrow your Swiss Army knife, promising to return it. You say "No way, Buster," remembering how he borrowed your Chipmunks album and left it in the sun; and then, when you got mad, he had the audacity to claim the album actually was his!

But your smooth-talking brother persists. He says he'll write a note that states he promises to return the Swiss Army knife to you after he returns from summer camp. Recalling the condition of your album after he borrowed it, you demand he back up his note by letting you keep his sack of marbles as collateral. He includes a clause to that effect in the note. You sign it, your brother signs it and, just to play it safe, you have Mom sign it, too.

You have just executed a deed of trust, secured by real property. You are the beneficiary (creditor) of the note. Your brother is the trustor (borrower), and your mother is trustee.

The terms "mortgage" and "deed of trust" are used interchangeably, though they are not the same thing. The difference between a mortgage and a deed of trust lies in how a foreclosure is executed if the borrower defaults. The use of mortgage or deed of trust varies from state to state. In California, trust deeds are used almost exclusively. A deed of trust involves the three parties outlined above. The deed of trust, executed by the creditor to secure an obligation (usually a promissory note), is a recorded lien on the property.

Only if the borrower defaults on the promissory note does the trustee become involved. The trustee may be any "legal person" (I'm not sure just what that means), although it typically is the title company used to insure the title. In the event you default on the loan, the trustee may sell the property at a "trustee's sale" and apply the proceeds of the sale to satisfy the debt. Promise you'll never learn about foreclosure proceedings first hand.

Should you one day own the property free and clear, there will be no more deeds of trust recorded on the property, only a "deed" in your name.

"Closing" is the final phase of a home purchase. Final papers are signed and recorded, and money changes hands, all done through escrow. The costs that the seller and buyer incur at this time are called "closing costs." Closing costs include appraisal fee, realtor's commission, lender's charges, advance mortgage payment, hazard insurance payment, mortgage insurance, real estate taxes, and title and escrow fees. Local custom determines who, seller or buyer, pays for which costs.

For a detailed discussion of closing costs, get a copy of "Buying a Home? Don't Forget Those Closing Costs!," a free booklet available from lenders or from reference 42. A second free publication, "Understanding Closing and Title Costs," is available from reference 14.

Since you, the buyer, must typically pay the lender's charges (which could amount to thousands of dollars), you may ease the sting by taking advantage of a quirk in tax law. If you pay the loan fee by check, rather than allowing the lender to subtract it from the loan proceeds, the loan fee is fully tax deductible in the year of the sale. If the lender pays the loan fee by withholding it from the loan proceeds, the loan fee must be amortized over the life of the loan.

PART THREE

CREATIVE HOME BUYING

In Part One of this book, you solved an equation that determined the house price you could afford. What did you find? Were the results exciting or depressing? The following section is for those people who found they could barely afford to buy a closet. You can purchase a home even when conventional wisdom says you can't. The solution is simple. Use unconventional wisdom.

Conventional wisdom dictates you put 20% down and take out a "30-year, fixed-rate" mortgage from the local bank to cover the rest. This method was the mainstay of the housing industry for nearly half a century. It was safe, easy, and predictable. Then came 1980.

With interest rates soaring to 16% in 1980, only one of every six California families could qualify to purchase a median-priced home; the housing industry plummeted into the worst recession since the Depression. The beleaguered industry was kept afloat primarily because home buyers took matters into their own hands and began employing "creative financing" techniques to purchase their homes. The banking industry then followed suit by introducing their own forms of creative financing. As will be seen, most of the new methods are either more complicated or more risky for the buyer than the simple 30-year, fixed-rate mortgages. However, these unconventional methods of financing have put home buying within the grasp of millions of families who otherwise would be excluded by excessive home prices and interest rates.

Let's first investigate the creative financing techniques employed by the banking industry. Since a third of all new mortgages in 1986 were of this type, these techniques, thought to be avant garde in 1980, have now become mainstream.

BANKER'S CREATIVE HOME BUYING

Adjustable Rate Mortgages

When the interest rate crisis occurred during the early 1980s, financial institutions created a way to make a home loan more affordable. The banks began to tie the interest on a home loan to a variable index, like U.S. treasury bills. Onto this index the institutions tack a "margin" of 1 or 2%, and that determines the interest rate the borrower pays. The lender periodically (every year, for example) adjusts the interest charged the borrower to equal the index plus the margin. Because these loans are less risky for the lender (and more risky for the borrower), the interest rate on an "adjustable-rate mortgage" (ARM) is typically 2% lower than the interest rate on a fixed-rate mortgage. Two percent may sound inconsequential. However, by plugging a 2% lower interest rate into the equation in Figure 3, you discover a radical difference in the house price you can afford.

Adjustable-rate mortgages are composed of a baffling array of variables. And, just to guarantee total confusion, each bank adds its own peculiarities to these variables. Locating the "best" ARM requires either an MBA or a systematic approach. Let's try a systematic approach. Figure 12 lists three different ARMs. First we'll examine the various parameters that make up an ARM, and then compare the three ARMs to determine which is best.

Figure 12. Adjustable-Rate Mortgage Table

	Bank A[1]	Bank B[1]	Bank C[2]
Initial interest rate	8%	7%	6%
Points	2	3	3
Index	C.O.F.	6 mo. T.B.	6 mo. T.B.
Margin	2%	2%	2%
Lifetime adjustment cap	5%	5%	6%
Rate adjustment period	1 yr.	6 mo.	6 mo.
Cap per adjustment	2%	1%	1%

[1] No negative amortization.

[2] Possible negative amortization. Payment adjusts annually. No note adjustment cap. Initial note rate of 7%.

Like fixed-rate loans, these loans are fully amortized 30-year loans. At the end of each adjustment period, the loan payment is adjusted so the loan is paid off 30 years from the loan origination date. As stated earlier, the institution tacks a "margin " of 1 or 2% onto the index, and that is the interest rate the borrower is charged. For example, the week this chart was drawn, the regional cost of funds (C.O.F.) was at 6%. Since Bank A adds a 2% spread to this 6%, its initial interest rate is 8%, as shown in Figure 12.

To make these adjustable loans more appealing to borrowers, banks have built certain safeguards into the loans. One safeguard is a limit ("cap") on the amount the interest may change over the life of the loan. The consumer is further protected by an adjustment cap, which limits the amount the interest may adjust at one time.

So which of the three adjustable loans in Figure 12 is best? Let's first compare Bank A to Bank B. The initial interest rate of Bank B seems lower by 1%. However, notice they charge an extra 1% loan-initiation fee (point). This loan-initiation fee is a one-time fee charged the borrower for the privilege of using the bank's money. Therefore, the lower interest rate of Bank B is offset by a higher initial fee. Bank B has a lower adjustment cap. But Bank B adjusts the payment every six months, yielding an annual adjustment cap of 2%, just like Bank A. Both banks indicate a life cap of 5%. The maximum interest rate of Bank A is therefore 13%, while the maximum interest rate of Bank B is 12%.

A six-month T-Bill index is more volatile than a cost of funds index. The more volatile the index, the riskier the loan is for the borrower. Typically, an index that adjusts every six months tends to fluctuate more than an index that adjusts annually. However, upon talking to the two lenders, Bank B reveals that it averages the T-Bill rate from the preceding six months and uses that figure as an index. Bank A, in contrast, doesn't average. Its index is the cost of funds on the change date. Therefore, the stability normally associated with the C.O.F. index is reduced.

Although the numbers between Bank A and B appear radically different, in the final analysis the only significant difference lies in the lifetime cap of the loan. Since Bank B has a lifetime cap 1% lower than

Bank A, it is the better of the two.

Now in reviewing Bank C we come upon a new term, "negative amortization." Recall that "amortization" means the remaining loan balance decreases with each payment. Negative amortization means that the amount of money owed the bank may actually increase over the life of the loan. This is because the interest rate of the "note" may be higher than the interest rate you pay.

For example, let's say you borrow $100 from a friend for one year. The interest rate she charges you is 24%, interest only. So over the course of the year she will charge you $24.00, payable in monthly installments of $2.00. However, since she's a nice person, she says that during the year you need only pay her at 12% interest, or $1.00 per month. So the interest you are charged is 24%, yet over the one-year life of the loan you are only required to reimburse her at a rate of 12%. She adds the difference between the amount you are charged and the amount you actually pay to your loan balance. Therefore, at the end of the year, you owe her $112, or $12 more than you initially borrowed! This is negative amortization.

Most people shy away from negative amortization. However, I view it simply as "borrowing" a little more money each month to assist in making the monthly payment. This borrowed money is then added to the overall sum owed. There are two conditions under which negative amortization should be avoided: First, when the house is not appreciating in value at a rate that keeps pace with the potentially increasing loan balance, and second, when the initial down payment is less than 20%.

Returning to Figure 12, notice that Note 2 of Figure 12 states that there is no adjustment cap on Bank C's note. However, the table states that Bank C has an adjustment cap of 1%. What gives? The adjustment cap of 1% is a cap on the interest you pay. But there is no limit on the change in interest of the note, except for the 6% lifetime cap. The difference between what you pay and what you are charged is added to the loan balance, resulting in negative amortization. Furthermore, the note rate adjusts semiannually, but the payment rate adjusts annually. This can also be a source of negative amortization. Also, note 2 indicates an initial note rate of 7%. However, the table states an initial interest payment rate of 6%. Therefore, from the very start of the loan, you're incurring negative amortization.

To compare a loan with negative amortization to a loan without negative amortization, compare the interest you are <u>charged</u>, not the interest you are required to <u>pay</u>. If the notes seem comparable (i.e., the amounts charged seem comparable), you may prefer the one with negative amortization because the payments are lower.

In this case, the loan notes of both Bank B and Bank C carry an initial rate of 7%, and both banks use a six month T-Bill index. Recall the lifetime interest cap for Bank B is 12%. Bank C indicates a lifetime adjustment cap of 6%. Therefore, the maximum interest rate is 6% + 6% = 12%, the same as Bank B.

But let's call Bank C just to be sure. Upon doing so, we find that, yes, the lifetime rate adjustment cap is 6%, but that cap is based on the initial interest rate you are charged (7%), not on the initial interest rate you are required to pay (6%). So now the overall lifetime cap from Bank C is 7% + 6% = 13%, 1% higher than Bank B. This fact, combined with the fact that the <u>note</u> of Bank B has a per-adjustment cap of 1% whereas the <u>note</u> of Bank C has no adjustment cap, makes the choice clear. The loan from Bank B is best.

Although adjustable-rate mortgages may initially seem about as logical as the electoral college, the concepts eventually make sense. As an aid to comparing ARMs, Bay Area newspapers publish rate tables similar to the table in Figure 12. (Bay Area mortgage tables will be discussed further. Also, reference 98 will analyze your adjustable mortgage options, for a fee.)

If you can qualify for an adjustable-rate mortgage and a fixed-rate mortgage, which should you take? The theoretical answer to this question is simple. If, while you hold the loan, the interest rate on the adjustable loan averages lower than the interest rate of the fixed loan, the adjustable is better. However, it's impossible to predict future fluctuations in interest rates. Therefore, although the above theory is perfectly correct, it is also perfectly useless. A rule of thumb is, when interest rates are high (as in 1981), an adjustable mortgage is a better idea. When interest rates are low (as they are now), a fixed-rate mortgage is best. Keep in mind that conventional fixed-rate mortgages are not assumable but adjustables usually are. Therefore, if you plan to sell in the near future, an adjustable-rate mortgage is best. For further information, order "Handbook on Adjustable Rate Mortgages" from reference 20 or "A New ARM For Today's Home Buyer" from reference 92.

Although an adjustable-rate mortgage is riskier for the consumer, it is a straightforward way to decrease the interest initially paid to the bank, thus eliminating an enormous barrier to home ownership for many people.

Private Mortgage Insurance

Another barrier faced by today's home buyer is the 20% down payment required by lenders. For a median-priced home in the Bay Area, this amounts to over $30,000-a rather ominous figure. But homes are sold daily with less than 20% down. In fact, over half of today's home buyers put down less than 20%. With a basic understanding of how lending institutions do business, you will see where the 20% figure originated, and how to avoid it.

Most lenders don't retain in their portfolios the loans they initiate. Usually loans are sold on the "secondary" market to investors. The lender continues to service the loan by sending statements and collecting payments. However, the payments are sent by the initiating lender to the investor who bought the loan. For this service the lender receives an annual fee from the investor. The two largest buyers of home loans are the Federal National Mortgage Association and the Federal Home Loan Mortgage Corporation, known in cutesy banker talk as Fannie Mae and Freddie Mac, respectively. These corporations are federally chartered but privately owned.

Both companies buy only loans which fall within their strict guidelines. As a result, many lenders structure their loan packages to meet the criteria of Fannie Mae and Freddie Mac. FNMA and FHLMC have decreed they will buy loans that exceed 80% of the purchase price. However, they stipulate that in such cases the buyer must obtain "private mortgage insurance" (PMI). This PMI insures the lender against possible losses should the homeowner default on the mortgage. Private mortgage insurance costs home buyers an additional .25 to .4% over their regular interest rate. If PMI is required, the lender will request that the insurance premium be included every month with the regular principal and interest payment. The loan papers should specify that PMI will no longer be required once the loan balance falls below 80% of the home value (either due to appreciation or due to a decreased loan balance).

Incidently, Fannie Mae has a maximum gross income to "PITI" (principal, interest, taxes, and insurance) ratio of 28%. That is why, in Part One, 28% was used in determining what house a buyer could afford. In an attempt to reduce the number of foreclosures on houses carrying low down payments, Fannie Mae recently changed its policy regarding qualification. When the down payment is between 5% and 10% (5% is FNMA's minimum), Fannie Mae requires that the PITI payments be less than 25% of your gross monthly income (as opposed to 28%).

A question often asked regarding downpayment is, "Shouldn't I put down as much as possible, so I don't have to pay so much interest to a bank?" There are pros and cons to a large down payment. Here are a few points to consider:

In favor of a large down payment:

1) When the interest rate on the loan is greater than the interest rate you are earning on your money, a large down payment is indicated. For example, if you are collecting 7% interest on your investments, then that is the cost of investing that money in a down payment. If the bank is charging 9% on the loan, then that is the cost of not investing that money in a down payment, and instead borrowing more from the bank. So, in this example, the cost of investing in a down payment is less than the cost of borrowing from the bank.

2) A larger down payment may allow you to avoid PMI premium payments. On a $100,000 loan, PMI could cost $400 annually. However, not all lenders sell to Fannie Mae and Freddie Mac, and therefore may allow a down payment as low as 10% without requiring PMI.

In favor of a low down payment:

1) A large loan that can be assumed by a subsequent buyer helps tremendously when you sell.

2) The peace of mind afforded by a safety net in the bank for emergencies or other investments suggests a low down payment.

3) When the interest the lender is charging is less than the interest you are making on your money, a low down payment is indicated.

Fifteen-Year Mortgages

To make monthly loan payments affordable, recall that lenders amortize fixed-rate loans over 30 years. However, with the recent fall in interest rates, lenders have discovered many home buyers qualify for loans amortized over fewer years. Because the loan must be repaid over fewer years, the monthly loan payments are higher than for a 30-year loan. However, since there are fewer years of interest payments, the overall interest paid to the lender is less. So for those home buyers who can qualify for the larger monthly payments, a reduced mortgage life represents thousands of dollars in savings.

Most lenders offer 15-year mortgages. These mortgages are not "creative" in the strict sense, because they are more difficult, not less difficult, to qualify for. But if you can qualify for the loan amount you need, a 15-year mortgage renders some savings over the long term.

As an example, let's examine a 15-year and a 30-year mortgage of $100,000. We will compare the two loans after 15 years of mortgage payments. The interest on a 15-year mortgage is typically 1/2% lower than a 30-year mortgage. As shown in Figure 13, the 30-year mortgage carries an interest rate of 10%, while the interest rate on the 15-year mortgage is 9.5%. Note that the gross monthly income required to qualify for the 15-year mortgage is indeed greater than for the 30-year mortgage. To make the comparison fair, assume the self-disciplined 30-year borrower invests the money saved by the lower mortgage payments. This amounts to $1,992 annually, and earns an after-tax interest rate of 6.5%.

After the 15-year mark, the 15-year borrower has paid about $68,000 more than the 30-year borrower. However, the 30-year borrower still owes the bank almost $82,000. The 15-year borrower, on the other hand, owes nothing. The loan is completely paid off. All things considered, the 15-year borrower fairs better than the 30 year borrower by about $14,000, saving approximately $1,000 per year over the 15-year period.

Note that the net cost of the 30-year mortgage would be much greater if the 30-year borrower did not

Figure 13. Comparison of the Cost of a 15–Year and a 30–Year Fully Amortized $100,000 Mortgage After 15 Years

		30 Year	15 Year
A.	Interest rate	10	9.5
B.	Monthly payments	$ 878	$ 1,044
C.	Gross monthly income required to qualify	3,200	3,800
	Loan balance after:		
D.	1 year	99,444	96,813
E.	5 years	96,574	80,606
F.	10 years	90,938	49,407
G.	15 years	81,665	0
	Total after 15 years:		
H.	Interest payments	139,705	87,920
I.	Tax deductions[a]	39,117	24,618
J.	After-tax interest income on $1,992/year (see text)	23,406	0

15–year summary:	30 Year	15 Year
Total money paid[b]	158,040	187,920
Tax savings (I)	−39,117	−24,618
Interest income (J)	−23,406	−0
Net money paid	95,517	163,302
Loan balance (G)	+81,665	+0
Net paid plus remaining liability	$ 177,182	$ 163,302

[a]Tax deductions = H x .28.

[b]Total money paid = B x 12 x 15.

make the annual deposits of $1,992 over the fifteen years. In this respect, a 15-year mortgage may be considered a forced savings account. Many prominent banks and real estate journalists have touted 15-year mortgages as rendering savings as much as $100,000. These new mortgages do provide some savings, but not nearly as much as consumers have been led to believe. For further details, request "How a 15-Year Mortgage Can Help You Save for the Future" from reference 92.

Mortgage Shopping

A house is probably not the most expensive item you'll ever purchase. The most expensive item you'll ever purchase is a mortgage. Over its life, a loan costs two or three times the price tag of a house. Hunt for financing with the same care and consideration you give your housing search.

An average-priced home may be magically transformed into a bargain with the right financing package. Unfortunately, lenders offering cut-rate financing aren't grouped together in the phone book. Furthermore, a bargain basement one week may be Gump's the next. Locating factory-outlet financing is not a question of where you look, but rather how you look.

The pain of mortgage shopping has been eased in the past few years by the proliferation of mortgage rate surveys. These surveys outline the loan origination fees and interest rates of a number of lenders. For adjustable-rate mortgages, these tables also specify the features indicated in Figure 12. Many local papers print mortgage tables every week, as shown in Figure 11. Mortgage surveys are also available from references 75 through 78.

The primary problem with mortgage surveys is that most lenders do not guarantee (or "lock in") their interest rate upon receipt of the loan application. Typically, the interest rate is locked in when the loan is approved, which may be four to eight weeks after the application is submitted. So a lender may lower its rate, receive a flood of applications, and then raise its rate again before it approves any loans.

You may protect yourself from this abusive treatment in three ways. First, always ask if the terms of the loan are locked in upon receipt of the application, and ask when the lock-in period expires. If the loan terms are guaranteed upon application, be sure to get that agreement in writing. The lender may increase the interest rate or charge extra points in exchange for this lock-in provision, which in turn decreases the value of the guarantee. A guaranteed rate is less crucial when interest rates are stable or declining.

A second defense against the banker's whims is to apply to lenders with consistently low rates. If a lender's rates are low week after week, a lock-in provision becomes less important. Determine which lenders are consistently low by monitoring a number of mortgage surveys for a few weeks.

To reduce the chance of becoming another notch in a banker's mahogany desk, apply to three lenders. This third technique will cost you more in the short term (nonrefundable application fees are about $200 to $300), but may save you thousands of dollars in the long term. In this way, you will not be victimized by a bank that processes your loan with the same urgency that the IRS returns your tax refund. Nor will you be left without alternatives should the lender increase the interest rate at the last moment.

The difficulty of comparing adjustable-rate mortgages is supposedly reduced by the "Truth-in-Lending" Act, which requires lenders to inform borrowers of the "annual percentage rate" (APR). In addition to the simple interest rate, the APR takes into account all initiation fees paid to the lender. As such, APRs should provide a more accurate representation of the true interest rate. Unfortunately, two lenders may offer the exact same loan package and arrive at APR figures that differ by as much as 2%. Yet both methods of APR calculation seem to fall within the guidelines specified by the Truth-in-Lending Act. The primary problem is some lenders consider possible future fluctuations in the interest rates, and others do not. Therefore, the APR is unfortunately a meaningless tool for comparing loans of different lenders.

One final note on mortgage shopping. In general, fixed-rate loans that carry bargain interest rates have higher loan-initiation fees. But over time, the higher initial fee is compensated for by the lower rate. For example, loan A carries an interest rate 1/2% lower than loan B. But loan A's loan-initiation fee is 1½ points higher than loan B. If you anticipate remaining in the house more than three years, loan A is the better choice.

As a guide to mortgage shopping, Figure 14 offers a list of questions to ask the lender about any given loan.

Figure 14. Questions to Ask About Mortgages

Questions relevant to both fixed and adjustable mortgages:

1. What is the interest rate?
2. What is the loan initiation fee?
3. Is the loan assumable at the original terms?
    How many times may it be assumed and what is the assumption fee?
4. What is the prepayment penalty?
5. Is PMI required?
    Once the loan balance falls below 80% of the house value, is PMI waived?
6. Is the rate locked in upon application?
    When does the rate guarantee period expire?
    What if the period expires as the result of the lender's delays?
7. What are the estimated closing costs?
                        (continued)

Figure 14 (continued)

Questions relevant only to adjustable mortgages:
8. Can the loan be converted to a fixed-rate mortgage?
    Is there a conversion fee or other restrictions?
9. Is negative amortization possible?
10. What is the initial interest rate?
11. Is there an initial interest discount?
    How might the interest rate change once the discount period expires?
12. What is the lifetime cap on the interest rate?
13. What is the adjustment cap?
14. What is the index?
    What is the adjustment period? An index that adjusts annually is usually better than one with a shorter adjustment period. Ask the lender to show you a chart depicting the three-year history of the index.
15. What margin is added to the index to determine the interest rate?
16. Is there a carry-over provision allowing the lender to counter the adjustment cap?
    If the interest rises more than the cap allows, these sneaky provisions allow the lender to carry over the extra unpaid interest and tack it onto next year's bills.

The lender should show you the answers to these questions in the loan documents.

PEOPLE'S CREATIVE HOME BUYING

All the preceding methods of reducing the cost of home purchase—obtaining an adjustable mortgage, insuring a low down payment with PMI, obtaining a 15-year mortgage, and careful comparative shopping—have become well-established practices in the 1980s. How-

ever, none of these methods may be sufficient if:
(1) you don't have enough money for a down payment or
(2) you don't have enough income to qualify for an institutional loan. These cases call for more radical purchase techniques. In fact, even if you can qualify for
an institutional loan, creative financing may yield a
better deal.

The Low Down

Aside from obtaining PMI, what are other methods
of buying a home with minimal down payment? We will
examine four methods of buying with a low down payment: (1) VA loans, (2) FHA loans, (3) lease with option
to buy, and (4) shared equity. This is by no means an
exhaustive list of how to purchase property with little
cash. The sources listed in the reference section can
give further details.

The Veteran's Administration and Federal Housing
Administration (which is a subdivision of the US Housing and Urban Development Department) both provide
insurance to the lender in the event you default on your
loan. Neither of the agencies actually supply the
money, which is obtained through mortgage brokers.

VA loans have some advantages over FHA loans.
On loans up to $110,000, the VA doesn't require a down
payment on the house; they provide 100% financing.
FHA loans, on the other hand, require about a 5% down
payment. Furthermore, the VA has a higher loan limit,
$135,000 as opposed to a $90,000 limit on FHA loans.
The charge for the VA loan guarantee is 1% of the total
loan, whereas the FHA charges 3.8% for their loan
insurance. A disadvantage of VA loans is they are only
available to veterans, although anyone may assume a
VA loan.

As mentioned earlier, most fixed-rate mortgages
are not assumable by subsequent buyers. However, both
VA and FHA loans are fully assumable. A disadvantage
of both VA and FHA loans is that you must wait

patiently while bureaucratic wheels slowly turn. The
sluggish government gears may be greased if the lender
has "auto approval" authority from the VA or "direct
endorsement" authority from the FHA. Both agencies
require the mortgage insurance premium to be paid
when the loan is originated, as opposed to paying the
premium in monthly installments, as with PMI. This
can be a substantial chunk of money. Figure 15
summarizes FHA and VA loans.

Figure 15. FHA and VA Loan Specifications

	FHA	VA
Loan limit for single-family home	$ 90,000	$ 135,000
Down payment	Note 1	Note 2
Loan guarantee fee (paid by borrower to FHA or VA)	3.8% Note 3	1%
Lender's fee (paid by borrower to lender)	1%	1%
Discount points (Note 4) (paid to lender)	Note 5	Note 6
Qualifying ratios (Note 7)		
Housing expense ratio	Note 8	--
Long-term debt ratio	Note 9	Note 10
Residual income	--	Note 11

Notes:
1: 3% of the first $25,000. 5% of the loan amount
   above $25,000.
2: 0% of the first $110,000. 25% of the loan amount
   above $110,000.
3: This loan guarantee fee is returned to borrower on
   a pro-rated basis upon selling.
4: Discount points are fees the lender charges to offset a lower (i.e. discount) interest rate.
5: The interest is not set by FHA. If a below-market
   rate is desired, then discount points are negotiated
   between lender and borrower.
                    (continued)

(Notes to Figure 15, continued)

6: The interest rate is set by the VA. To offset the difference between current market rates and VA limits, the lender charges discount points. The seller is required by the VA to pay these points.

7: The qualifying guidelines of both the VA and FHA are very elastic. Every rule has an exception. This chart doesn't list all the qualifying considerations. See a lender for the full story.

8: Gross monthly income - federal income tax = net effective income. Housing expenses ratio = PITI/net effective income $\leq 38\%$.

9: (PITI + long-term debts) / (net effective income - state income tax -FICA) $\leq 53\%$.

10: (PITI + long term debts) / GMI $\leq 41\%$.

11: Net effective income - state income tax - FICA - PITI - long-term debts - maintenance - utilities = residual income. This residual income must be greater than a value from a VA chart. For example, for two people the residual income must be $697 or greater. See a lender for details.

The third method of getting into a house for little up-front cash is the short term lease with an option to buy. For some "consideration for the option" money (usually between $1,000 to $5,000), the seller gives you the option to purchase the house when the lease expires. An agreed-upon portion of the monthly rent payment is applied toward the purchase price if the option is exercised. The option-consideration money is also applied toward the purchase. Until the option is exercised, the seller remains the legal owner, making the mortgage payments, with the aid of your monthly rental payment. You do not receive any of the tax write-off benefits until you actually purchase the house.

Note that the lease-option method doesn't lower the down payment, but it does delay the down payment by a few years. In addition to delaying the down payment, the lease option affords three advantages over other methods of home purchase. First, you can test out the house before you decide to purchase. Many home buyers, sitting under a leaking roof, wish they had had this luxury. Second, the lease option ties up a home for two or three years while you improve your financial standing. Third, you lock in the cost of the home now, so there are no surprises two or three years down the road. The agreement specifies an annual increase in the house price to cover appreciation, but often you can negotiate an appreciation figure lower than the actual appreciation.

Homes are usually not advertised as "lease-option" deals, so you, the buyer, must broach the subject with the seller. Good candidates for lease options are houses that have been on the market for a while and houses that were formally rentals. The supreme advocate of lease options is Bob Bruss. Further information can be found in his book (reference 4) or by ordering report #85129 ($3.50) from reference 19.

The fourth means of purchasing a house for no cash is to have someone else pay the down payment. A person willing to pay your down payment is either a business man or someone who loves you very, very much. I suggest getting it from the latter. This brings Mom and Dad to mind. But don't call up Mom and say, "Gee, I want to buy a house; can I have $10,000?" Call and say, "I have a shared-equity investment opportunity I would like to discuss with you." Better ask to speak with Dad; for some reason males get excited by terms like "shared equity."

Shared equity creates a symbiotic relationship between someone with a good income but little savings (you) and someone with a good income and a lot of savings (Mom and Dad).

It works like this: Your parents pay the entire down payment. You and your parents decide how to split the interest in the property (50/50, 60/40, etc.).

Your parents are the "investors/co-owners." They do not live in the house. You are the "resident/co-owner." You live in the house. You and your parents pay proportional parts of the interest, taxes, and insurance. In addition, you pay rent to your parents for their portion of the house which you are using. If their share is 50%, you pay them 50% of fair-market rent.

So you've gotten into a house with no down payment, but what do your parents get from this? Along with the rental income, they get two tax write-offs. First, they can deduct their portion of the interest and taxes, just like you. But they can also deduct "depreciation" on their interest in the house that is rented to you. This added tax advantage could potentially repay their entire down payment. For $3.50 you can receive report #85131 from reference 19, which further details shared equity, as does Georgia Anderson's book (reference 2).

Incidently, if your parents try to pull the old "but tax reform eliminated tax write offs for investors" trick, reassure them that their tax write-off is of utmost concern to you. Explain that if income on their joint return is below $100,000, they may write off up to $25,000 in depreciation. Also, they may deduct interest payments up to $10,000 over and above the income from the investment. Not only are they now reassured, but they are also very impressed by your sound business knowledge.

If your parents are moved to actually give you the down payment (after all, you did let them live with you for eighteen years), then have the down payment transferred to your account two months prior to applying for a loan. Fannie Mae requires that at least five percent of the house cost be your own money. Fannie Mae defines "your own money" as money that has been in your account at least two months.

Obtaining a Loan When the Banker Says You Can't

The down payment is not the only obstacle you face as a first-time home buyer. You must also meet the bank's demand that the monthly mortgage payments absorb less than 28% of your monthly income. If you find you can't qualify for the amount of financing you need, you have four options: (1) Pool your resources with others so you can qualify. (2) Buy something less expensive. (3) Borrow from a lender that employs less restrictive qualifying guidelines. (4) Borrow from a lender that has lower interest rates.

One or more of these four options are encompassed by each of the following ten methods of home purchase: (1) co-signer, (2) shared ownership, (3) condominium, (4) foreclosure, (5) pre-market purchase, (6) friends and relatives, (7) seller finance, (8) loan assumption, (9) FHA/VA, (10) government bonds. We will examine each of these briefly.

If you discover a loan package that suits your needs but you can't meet the qualifying requirements, you may consider obtaining a co-signer on the loan. The bank applies its qualifying ratios to the combined incomes of the primary borrower and the co-signer, thereby making it easier for you to qualify for the loan. Be aware that the lender typically requires the co-signer to sign the deed of trust also. By signing the loan papers with you, the co-signer acts as an insurance policy on the loan. Should you default, the lender will require the co-signer to continue the loan payments. The co-signer must state on subsequent loan applications that she or he has co-signed a loan. They may therefore find it difficult to obtain a loan while co-signed on your loan. Essentially a co-signer becomes part owner of the mortgage, with all its associated obligations, without becoming part owner of the house, with all its associated benefits. This sort of martyrdom again suggests Mom and Dad.

The second method is to pool your resources with other people and share ownership of the house. Popularly known as "mingling," this method differs from the shared-equity method mentioned earlier in that all owners occupy the house. There is no "investor." The rule here is "good contracts make good co-owners." Even shared ownership between friends or relatives should be based on a sound contractual agreement. The issues that must be anticipated and spelled out in writing include how the mortgage and down payment are divided, how utilities and maintenance costs are shared, how each party may use the property, how the profits and tax benefits are to be shared, how sales decisions are to be made, and how to deal with a co-owner who cannot or will not meet his or her obligation to the property.

The contract also specifies how title is to be held. The two most popular arrangements are the "limited partnership" and the "tenancy in common agreement." Reference 5, The Partnership Book, includes a sample real-estate partnership agreement. Also, Robert Irwin's book (reference 7) is an excellent guide to mingling. Since there are no standard shared-ownership agreement forms, a real-estate attorney should be consulted in structuring the partnership contract.

Another shared housing avenue is the limited-equity cooperative. Typically, a co-op is created by a nonprofit community group or a group of tenants seeking to purchase their building. Structured to limit the profit members may may realize upon selling their shares, limited-equity cooperatives put home ownership within the reach of low-income people. References 69 through 74 provide assistance in the creation of cooperatives.

Both methods 1 and 2, securing a co-signer and shared ownership, are ways to qualify for a bank loan by pooling resources with others. Another avenue, when you encounter difficulty in qualifying for a bank loan, is to buy a cheaper home. The risk in buying a cheap home is that it may be even cheaper by the time you decide to sell. This is known, in sophisticated real estate jargon, as "a lousy deal." However, by observing certain precautions, you can minimize the inherent risk of buying an inexpensive home. We shall examine three sources of cheap homes: condominiums, foreclosures, and pre-market purchase.

The perils of purchasing a condominium are exemplified by the unfortunate experience of a friend of mine. Nancy found an ideal condo for herself—great financing, low down payment, beautifully designed, swimming pools, jacuzzi, sauna, and close to work.

As she was moving in, a neighbor came over to greet her. "You aren't actually moving in, are you?" questioned the neighbor, "Do you know what's going on here?"

Nancy then listened as the neighbor elaborated on one horror story after another. The builder had run into financial troubles. A third of the condominium complex would remain unfinished for an indefinite period of time. Of the two-thirds that was complete, the builder was renting the vacant units, instead of selling them (property values plummet if over 20% of the units are rented). Nancy asked if the lender might bail the builder out of this fix. No, because the finance company itself had just filed bankruptcy!

Nancy spoke to other members of the condominium. One resident after another told stories of inadequate sound insulation, noise from airplanes (the complex was built in the flight path of the local airport), swimming pools never completed, inadequate hot water (the water heaters were sometimes 100 feet from the units they serviced), poor mail service (the developer hadn't supplied mail boxes), and a long fight with the developer just to get lawn furniture for one of the outdoor common areas. When she asked one resident what he was going to do, the answer was simple: "Move as soon as possible."

You can avoid Nancy's dilemma by doing a little research prior to purchasing a condominium. The primary complaint of condominium owners is poor construction, especially inadequate sound proofing between adjoining condos. To check the building's insulation, ask neighbors above, below, and to the sides to turn on a TV or stereo and listen from inside your unit. Also, ask the condo owner's association about any other structural problems. The owner's association can also provide you with their latest financial statement. Unless a portion of the monthly maintenance fee is set aside to cover emergencies, expect a large special assessment when a major repair becomes necessary. Because nonresident owners want to keep monthly fees at a minimum, maintenance quality decreases in direct proportion to the number of rented units. Carefully examine how well both the building and common area are maintained. In a new building, determine how many of the units have sold. As many frustrated Bay Area condo owners will testify, never be among the first buyers in a new complex. For every unit the developer still owns, the developer has one vote in the condo owner's association. Believe me, you do not want as a general partner in building maintenance and management a developer who is losing money. Furthermore, you do not want to compete with unsold new units when you decide to sell your condo. Condominiums make excellent starter homes, but thoroughly investigate the complex before you buy.

In addition to condominiums, foreclosed homes also provide an opportunity to puchase an inexpensive house. Recall that all lenders hold the property as collateral via a deed of trust. In the event a borrower fails to make the mortgage payments, the lender can repossess the property.

There are three time periods during which distressed property may become available for purchase. The first time is after the Notice of Default has been filed against the borrower. After the Notice of Default has been filed, the borrower has three months (in California) to reinstate the mortgage. To reinstate the loan, the borrower must make up any missed loan payments and pay any trustee fees and expenses. During this period, the borrower may very well wish to sell the property, often at a discount.

To find borrowers in this unfortunate quandary, contact the county clerk who records notices of mortgage default. In urban areas, this information may be obtained by subscribing to a local public recording summary service. The county clerk or a title insurance firm can tell you if such a service exists in your area.

The second opportunity to purchase foreclosed property is at the foreclosure sale. These sales require the buyer put up full cash payment, and therefore are of little interest to first-time home buyers.

The final opportunity to purchase foreclosed property is after the foreclosure sale. If there are no bidders at the foreclosure sale, the lender takes title to the property. The repossessed property which the lender holds is called REO (real estate owned). Most lenders are anxious to get rid of these properties and sell them at very favorable terms. Contact each lender's REO officer. Ask if they presently hold any REOs, and request that you be notified as new properties become available. Follow up this conversation with a note to the REO officer, restating your interest in buying a foreclosed property. It may take some doing to get the lender to take you seriously, but persistence pays.

The US Housing and Urban Development Department publishes its repossessed homes weekly in the classified section of the Sunday Examiner. The newspaper announcement also explains how to bid on these houses. Call the VA near the beginning of the month for a list of their repossessed homes. For information on Fannie Mae foreclosures, see reference 93. Furthermore, all the agencies in the reference section which provide government-sponsored loans also hold repossessed homes.

Condominiums are less expensive because they are cheaper to build and less desirable to own. Foreclosures are less expensive because they are more difficult to buy and unwanted by the sellers. But what about houses that are less expensive because they are simply a good deal? Part Two described some bargain-hunting tricks. Let's explore one source of bargains not touched upon in Part Two: buying a house before it is put on the market. By purchasing before the property is advertised, you've automatically eliminated all your competition and bypassed realtors and their commissions. Within the limits set by the seller, you can write your own ticket.

To find a house before it is advertised, you must either find someone who is about to sell or someone who can be persuaded to sell. To locate someone thinking of selling a home, your best avenue is good old word of mouth. Let it be known to friends and relatives that you are in the market. Ask your doctor, banker, hair cutter, or dentist if they know of a potential seller. It is, unfortunately, a hit-and-miss method.

However, locating someone who may be persuaded to sell a home is not as hit and miss. Landlords are ripe potential sellers, waiting to be harvested. For starters, if you like the house in which you presently live, ask your landlord about buying it. All landlords live in the shadow of monthly mortgage payments just like homeowners. When rental owners receive 30-days notice from tenants, they may not be able to afford the lost rental income while waiting for the property to sell. Therefore, they simply put the home back on the rental market. However, if you approach them at this time, while they are hassling with new paint jobs and finding new tenants, they may be very willing to wash their hands of the whole mess and sell to you. Rental ads are overflowing with owners in this exact quandary. Call on homes that interest you and ask the landlord if he or she would consider selling.

Furthermore, property owners associations are comprised of disgruntled landlords bound together by their common hatred of rent control. These associations all have newsletters in which you may place an ad announcing your interest in buying a house. The California Apartment Association (reference 88) can direct you to property owners associations in your area. Also, by rummaging through the public files at the Berkeley, Oakland, or San Francisco rent boards, you may determine which rental owners recently faced legal battles with tenants. A landlord who is reeling from a recent court skirmish might love to get rid of the property.

All the remaining sources of home loans to be examined embrace both liberal qualifying guidelines and lower interest rates. Even if you can qualify for a conventional bank loan, the following five financing schemes should be investigated. They might save you thousands of dollars.

Wouldn't it be fun to send your monthly mortgage payment to friends and relatives instead of some cold, impersonal bank? You can do just that, and create a fantastic deal for all parties in the process. By tapping friends and relatives for financing, you avoid the restrictive qualifying policies of conventional lenders and you bypass the bank's loan-initiation fee. Furthermore, you can often agree to a below-market interest rate. And the person lending you money usually earns a higher interest than the bank pays. But all your friends are misers? You may be surprised. A friend who is hesitant to lend you $200 for a vacation may be happy to lend you $20,000 for a house, if the loan is secured by a deed of trust. I financed the entire construction of my home in this manner.

A more likely source of financing is the seller of the property. Seller financing affords the same benefits of borrowing from friends, but avoids all the nasty situations that can arise when mixing friendship and money. In 1984, seller financing accounted for almost

40% of all new mortgages. The seller financing trend is exciting for the same reason the for-sale-by-owner trend is exciting. It is people taking control of their own financial dealings by eliminating institutions and middle men. It allows the buyer and seller to write their own terms, not just accept the terms dictated by a bank.

Seller financing will be illustrated with an example. Joan wants to buy a house and has $10,000 to apply toward a down payment. David is approaching retirement and has owned his home for 20 years. He wants to sell his urban home and buy a house in the country. His original mortgage, executed in 1967 at 6% interest, has an $8,000 balance remaining.

Joan purchases the house for $100,000. She puts down $10,000. If Joan were to obtain a conventional 30-year, fixed-rate bank loan, she would need an annual salary of nearly $35,000 in order to qualify. Furthermore, she would need to pay a loan-initiation fee of nearly $2,500.

But David agrees to finance the sale himself. He uses part of the down payment to pay off the $8,000 first deed of trust. He then "carries back" a $90,000 note, secured by a new first deed of trust on the property. He and Joan agree to a 9% interest-only loan, with the balloon payment of $90,000 due in five years. Figure 16 illustrates the transaction. Note that although Joan has a $90,000 "loan" from David, he has not actually handed her any money. For David, it's as if he were paid the full $100,000 and immediately took $90,000 and put it in a five-year term account at 9% interest. For Joan, it's as if she got a $90,000 five-year loan from a bank at 9% interest, and immediatly paid the $90,000 to David. In five years, both Joan's income and the value of the house will have increased. She should have no trouble obtaining a new mortgage to pay off the balloon in five years. This is a good deal for both Joan and David.

Figure 16. Seller Financing Example

Purchase price	$ 100,000
Down payment	10,000
Amount financed by seller	$ 90,000
Purchase price	$ 100,000
Balance of existing mortgage	8,000
Money to seller[a]	$ 92,000

[a]This amount is not fully realized until the $90,000 note is paid off in five years by the buyer.

Now assume Joan initially encounters some resistance from David, because he needs more than $2,000 (=$10,000 - 8,000) cash out of the deal to help purchase his home in the country. This is not an uncommon occurrence with seller financing. But Joan really wants to purchase David's home and suggests that she assume the first deed of trust. To "assume" a loan means to take over the loan at the original terms and interest rate. In 1985, one of every six property purchases involved the assumption of an existing mortgage. A mortgage initiated in 1974 or earlier carries a fixed interest rate of 8.5% or lower.

If the present loan on the property does not contain a legally enforceable "due on sale" clause and the interest rate is favorable, you may want to assume the existing loan. A "due on sale" clause in the mortgage or deed of trust gives the lender the power to demand full payment of the loan if the property changes hands. A loan is "assumable" if the lender does not have that power. Most fixed-rate loans initiated today contain "due on sale" clauses. However, many loans executed before 1980 do not carry this stipulation. Most loans available through home mortgage revenue bonds are assumable. Neither FHA nor VA loans contain due on sale clauses. Also, any loan sold to Fannie Mae before

November 10, 1980, can be assumed at the original terms and interest rate. If asked, the lender is required to divulge if and when the loan was sold to Fannie Mae.

There are two ways to assume a loan. With both methods the buyer must complete the lender's loan assumption application. The first method involves paying an assumption fee and formally assuming the mortgage. The seller is then released from all obligation to the lender. The second method is to purchase the property "subject to" the existing loan. In this case the buyer does not formally assume the loan, and therefore no assumption fee is charged. However, the seller remains responsible for the loan in the eyes of the lender. For further information on assumable loans, order report #84124 ($3.50) from reference 19.

The ninth source of low-interest loans and liberal qualifying guidelines is the FHA and the VA. These agencies take into consideration much more than gross monthly income in determining the loan amount. As outlined in Figure 15, their qualifying ratios are much more liberal than conventional lenders. Furthermore, by paying extra loan-origination points, the interest rate may be bought down to below market rates. For example, by paying an additional 2 points, the lender may reduce the interest rate by $\frac{1}{2}$ percent.

Because your are a sensitive, caring person, concerned about the welfare of your fellow human beings, you have always voted in favor of state and local housing bond issues. Now is the time to reap what ye hath sown. City, county, and state agencies are overflowing with housing bond money, and they want to give it to you! Not only do they have money to hand you, but their qualification requirements are more liberal, their interest rates are lower, and they charge fewer points than conventional lenders. These loans are usually earmarked for median to low-income first-time home buyers.

Sometimes these bargain loans are fed into the community via developers who pass the loans on to the consumer. In other cases, the loans are available through conventional lenders for the consumer to use for either new or used home purchase. For example, the State of California has $242 million of mortgage revenue bond money to provide below-market interest rate loans to first-time home buyers. The fixed-rate interest on these 30-year assumable loans is 8.4%, and they finance up to 95% of the purchase. And, as if this isn't enough to make your calculator overheat, they allow a PITI-to-income ratio of 28% (as opposed to the 25% ratio of conventional lenders). The references list a number of bond revenue sources. To find similar agencies in other areas, look under "Housing and Community Development Department" in the government listing section of the phone book.

Well, are you feeling overwhelmed? Does home purchase seem like such a monumental task that you would rather not think about it? Purchasing a home on a tight budget requires common sense, patience, research, and ingenuity. And you can do it! The reference section at the end of this book lists many channels for acquiring both knowledge and financing. And it only scratches the surface of the total resources available.

Unfortunately, despite all the seller financing, adjustable-rate mortgages, and Fannie Maes, this country is in the throes of a serious crisis in housing. In 1981, President Reagan's Commission on Housing found one of every ten households live in substandard housing. Families wait an average of two years to be allowed into tenement housing projects. Yet, since 1981, low-income housing assistance has been slashed by nearly seventy percent. And there are those who cannot even afford to rent a house in the slum. In California alone it is estimated that 100,000 people are homeless.

Luckily, there are organizations struggling with this crisis. The "Progressive Housing Alliance" advocates the housing needs of low-income people at the state capitol. On a national level, the "National Low-

Income Housing Coalition" is fighting a losing battle with the administration to keep 50 years of housing programs from being gutted. Both these organizations need your support, and are listed in the resource section.

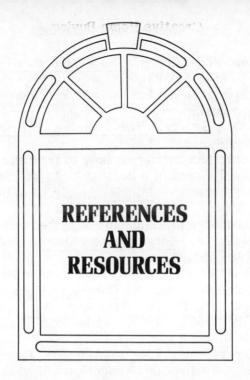

REFERENCES AND RESOURCES

Books:

1. Allen, Robert. <u>Nothing Down</u>. Simon & Schuster, 1984. $16.95.
   The "bible" of buying property with little cash.
2. Anderson and Lamb. <u>Equity Sharing</u>. Contemporary Books, 1986. $6.95.
   Explains the pros and cons of shared equity, and includes sample shared-equity contracts.
3. Bregman and Miller. <u>Buyer's Brokerage: A Practical Guide for Real Estate Buyers, Brokers, and Investors</u>. Tremont Press, PO Box 2307, Silver Spring, Maryland 20902. (301) 649-6666. 1986. $6.95.
   Short but thorough explanation of "buyer's brokers" real estate agents.
4. Bruss, Robert. <u>Smart Investor's Guide to Real Estate</u>. Crown Publishers, 1985. $15.95.
   Great source of information on conventional and unconventional financing written by one of the sharpest people in the field.

5. Clifford and Warner. The Partnership Book. Nolo Press, 1986. $17.95.

   Appropriate for those considering shared ownership.

6. Hoffman, George. How to Inspect a House. Addison Wesley, 1985. $8.95.

   Excellent primer on how to scrutinize the physical aspect of a home prior to purchasing.

7. Irwin, Robert. Mingles. McGraw-Hill, 1984. $15.95.

   Thorough investigation of shared ownership.

8. Jones, Peter. House Hunters Diary. Dell Publishing, 1985. $3.95.

   Must reading for any first-time home buyer.

9. Mc Cormack, Don. Mc Cormack's Guides. Donnan Publications, PO Box 773, Martinez, Calif. 94553. (415) 229-3581. 1987. $4.50 (plus $1.52 tax and shipping).

   Irreverent guides to Alameda, Contra Costa, and Santa Clara counties. Includes school rankings, crime statistics, and city profiles. Specify county of interest.

10. Money magazine editors. Money Guide: Your Home. Andrews, McMeel and Parker, 1986. $6.95.

    Excerpts from Money magazine. Covers home buying, remodeling, selling, financing and much more.

11. Realty Blue Book. Professional Publishing Corporation, 122 Paul Drive, San Rafael, Calif. 94903. (415) 472-1964. 1987. $22.00.

    Includes realty finance tables, purchase offer clauses, explanations of various mortgage instruments and much more.

Free or Inexpensive Real Estate Publications:

12. Bank of America, local branches.

    There are four "Consumer Information Reports" of interest to home buyers: 1. Steps to Buying a Home, 2. A Guide to Selling Your

Home, 3. Planning Home Improvements,
4. Shopping for Adjustable Rate Credit.
13. California Association of Realtors, PO Box 76917,
Los Angeles, Calif. 90076. (213) 739-8227.
Request 1987 Publications Catalog.
14. California Land Title Association, PO Box 13968,
Sacramento, Calif. 95853. (916) 444-2647.
Ask for their free pamphlet, "Understanding
Closing and Title Costs." Enclose a self-
addressed, stamped business-size envelope
with your request.
15. California Mortgage Bankers Association, 1127
Eleventh Street, Suite 534, Sacramento, Calif.
95814. (916) 446-7100.
Order their free pamphlet, "Choosing the
Mortgage That is Right For You," by sending a
stamped, self-addressed business-size
envelope. Their discussion of seller financing
is, of course, biased, but the rest is extremely
well written.
16. Center for Real Estate and Urban Economics, 2680
Bancroft Way, Suite A, University of California,
Berkeley, Calif. 94720. (415) 642-0224.
Ask for current publications list.
17. Contractors State Licensing Board, PO Box 26000,
Sacramento, Calif. 95826. (916) 366-5153.
Their free pamphlet, "Blueprint for Building
Quality," offers guides to choosing a contrac-
tor.
18. Cooperative Extension, University of California,
2120 University Avenue, Berkeley, Calif. 94720.
(415) 644-4345.
Ask for publications catalog. Brochures on
everything from shopping for loans to remov-
ing stains from fabric.
19. Newspaper Books, PO Box 4367, Orlando, Florida
32802-4367.
Ask to be sent "publication list" of Robert
Bruss' excellent reports.

-Federal Government Publications-

20. Consumer Information Center, PO Box 100, Pueblo, Col. 81002. (303) 948-3334.

    Request their catalog of consumer guides. Some publications are available which are unfortunately omitted from their guide. These include: "Handbook on Adjustable Rate Mortgages" (580P), free and "Mortgage Money Guide" (129R), $1.00.

21. Department of Housing and Urban Development, Program Information Center, 451 7th Street S.W., Room 1104, Washington, DC. 20401. (202) 755-6420.

    To experience Reagan's housing policies in action, try phoning HUD. They think they may have the following two free publications: "Let's Consider Cooperatives" and "Questions About Condominiums - What to Ask Before You Buy."

22. Federal Home Loan Bank Board, Information Office, Office of Public Affairs, 2nd Floor, 1700 G Street N.W., Washington, DC. 20552. (202) 377-6677.

    Publications on everything from co-ops to ARMs. Request publications list.

23. Federal Reserve Bank, Public Information, PO Box 7702, San Francisco, Calif. 94120. (415) 974-3231.

    Ask for publication list, "Public Information Materials."

24. Government Printing Office Bookstore, 450 Golden Gate Avenue, San Francisco, Calif. 94102. (415) 556-0642.

    Order "Homes" (subject bibliography #41), which lists government publications pertaining to housing.

Community Colleges and Adult Education:

The following community colleges offer a course entitled "Principles of Real Estate," which is appropriate for first-time buyers. In addition, their "Community Education Departments" occasionally hold seminars for first-time buyers.

Most Bay Area communities also have adult education programs that offer real estate seminars. Finding these adult schools in the phone book isn't easy. For example, in San Francisco they are listed in the government listings under "Schools -Colleges and Adult Education," whereas in Berkeley they are listed in the white pages under "Berkeley Public Schools."

The following list focuses on Bay Area Community College Districts (CCD).

25. Contra Costa CCD.
    Each campus has its own schedule and its own Community Services Department.
    > Contra Costa College, San Pablo. (415) 235-7800.
    > Diablo Valley College, Pleasant Hill. (415) 685-1230.
    > Los Medanos, Pittsburg. (415) 439-2181.

26. Chabot CCD. (415) 786-6600.
    Call district office for comprehensive schedule.
    > Chabot College, Hayward. (415) 786-6600.
    > Chabot College, Livermore. (415) 455-5300.

27. Foothill/DeAnza CCD.
    Class schedule covers both campuses. Community Services Department has its own schedule.
    > Community Services. (415) 960-4373.
    > DeAnza College, Cupertino. (408) 996-4760.
    > Foothill College, Los Altos Hills. (415) 960-4600

28. Fremont/Newark CCD.
    The Community Services Department schedule is listed in the regular schedule of classes.
    > Ohlone College, Fremont. (415) 659-6000.

29. Marin CCD.
    Class schedule and catalog is sent to all Marin residents. Community Education has a separate

schedule.

 Community Education. (415) 485-9305.

 College of Marin, Kentfield. (415) 485-9411.

30. Peralta CCD. (415) 466-7200.

Call their district office for a schedule covering all their campuses. Community Education courses are listed in the rear of the schedule.

 College of Alameda. (415) 522-7221.

 Merritt College, Oakland. (415) 531-4911.

 Vista College, Berkeley. (415) 841-8431.

31. San Francisco CCD. (415) 239-3070.

Their "centers," located throughout San Francisco, occasionally offer seminars in real estate. Call district office for a comprehensive schedule. City College has a separate schedule.

 San Francisco City College. (415) 239-3000.

32. San Jose CCD. (408) 274-6700.

Call district office for schedule covering both campuses.

 Evergreen College, San Jose. (408) 274-7900.

 San Jose City College. (408) 298-2181.

33. San Mateo County CCD.

Each campus has separate schedule. The Community Education schedule is also separate.

 Community Education. (415) 574-6563.

 Canada College, Redwood City. (415) 364-1212.

 San Mateo College. (415) 574-6161.

 Skyline College, San Bruno. (415) 355-7000.

34. West Valley Joint CCD. (408) 867-2200.

Call district office for comprehensive schedule. Community Development Department has a separate schedule.

 Community Development Department. (408) 867-0440.

 Mission College, Santa Clara. (408) 988-2200

 West Valley College, Saratoga. (408) 867-2200.

Workshops, Seminars, and Classes:

35. Castle Seminars, 3020 Bridgeway Blvd., Suite #166, Sausalito, Calif. 94965. (415) 388-6766.

    Offers seminars throughout the Bay Area for first-time buyers. $20 to $30 plus $8 material fee.

36. Learning Annex, 2500 Clay Street, San Francisco, Calif. 94115. (415)922-9900.

    Free guide includes real estate seminar listings.

37. Open Education Exchange Newspaper, PO Box 9654, Berkeley, Calif. 94709. (415) 526-7190.

    Free guide includes real estate seminar listings.

38. Owner Builder Center, 1516 Fifth Street, Berkeley, Calif. 94710. (415) 526-9222.

    Courses offered throughout the Bay Area on house building, renovation and remodeling.

39. San Francisco Lowry Investors Association, PO Box 26277, San Francisco, Calif. 94126. (415) 221-7171.

    Ask to be sent newsletter. Some workshops of interest to first-time buyers are open to nonmembers for a fee.

40. Stoklosa Seminars, c/o Grubb and Ellis Realty, 930 Santa Cruz Avenue, Menlo Park, Calif. 94025. (415) 323-7751.

    Free home-buying seminars that include a thorough discussion of "buyer's brokers."

41. UC Berkeley Extension, 2223 Fulton Street, Berkeley, Calif. 94720. (415) 642-4111.

    Offers many courses in both Berkeley and San Francisco on subjects ranging from partnerships to restoration.

Government Programs:

-Federal-

42. Dept. of Housing and Urban Development, 450 Golden Gate Avenue, San Francisco, CA 94102. (415) 556-5900.

    Ask for the general information packet on the Federal Housing Administration. The packet includes "Programs of HUD," a general booklet listing all of HUD's housing programs. Also included is information on FHA loans and closing costs. The classified section of the Sunday Examiner lists repossessed homes that HUD has for sale, and the information packet explains how to purchase HUD foreclosures.

43. Veterans Administration, 211 Main Street, San Francisco, Calif. 94105. (415) 495-8900.

    Ask for pamphlets 26-4, 26-5, and 26-6. Also ask for current list of VA repossessed homes.

44. Office of Historic Preservation, Dept. Parks and Recreation, PO Box 2390, Sacramento, Calif. 95811. (916)445-8006

    Information on qualifying for tax credits for rehabilitating historic buildings.

45. Farmers Home Administration, 194 Main Street, Suite F, Woodland, Calif. 95695-2915. (916) 666-3382.

    Provides home improvement and home purchase low-interest loans for families who can't qualify for conventional loans. Limited to rural communities of less than 10,000 people. Ask for the Rural Housing Section.

-State-

46. California Housing Finance Agency, 1121 L Street, 7th Floor, Sacramento, Calif. 95814. (916) 322-3991.

    Request list of lenders participating in the 1986 Home Mortgage Purchase Program.

These fixed-rate loans carry 8.4% interest rates and require 5% down. Qualifying ratio on these assumable loans is 28%/36%. Also, request list of developers participating in the Home Mortgage Purchase Program.

47. Cal-Vet, 2520 Stanwell Drive, Suite 160, Concord, Calif. 94520. (800) 952-5626.

These programs are different from VA loans. The interest rate varies over the life of the loan. It is currently at 7%. Also, Cal-Vet actually supplies the loan; they don't simply guarantee the loan.

48. Rural California Housing Corporation, 2125 19th Street, Suite 101 W, Sacramento, Calif. 95818. (916) 442-4731.

Works with the Farmers Home Administration assisting low-income home buyers to build their own homes in special rural housing projects.

–Local–

49. Alameda County Planning Dept., Housing and Community Development Program, 224 West Winton Avenue, Hayward, Calif. 94544. (415) 881-6094.

Ask for list of developers participating in 1985 Single Family Mortgage Revenue Bond Program. Assumable loans of 9-7/8% with 5% down and .75% loan origination fee.

50. Berkeley Housing Rehabilitation Office, 2180 Milvia Street, Berkeley, Calif. 94704. (415) 644-6590.

Rehabilitation "Section 312" loans are available up to $27,000 at interest rates of 3%, 6%, and 9%. Also request information on the Double Unit Opportunity Program, which assists home owners in adding second living units to their property.

51. Oakland Office of Community Development, 1417 Clay Street, Oakland, Calif. 94612. (415) 273-3502.

    Ask for fact sheet on single-family bond program (8.95% loans, 5% down, 5 points). For information on all the OCD programs, request the "1987 OCD Housing Programs" pamphlet.

52. Contra Costa County, PO Box 951, 651 Pine Street, Martinez, Calif. 94553. (415) 372-2006

    The Mortgage Revnue Bond Program provides loans of 10.15% interest with 5% down.

53. Contra Costa County, Neighborhood Preservation Program, PO Box 749, Martinez, Calif. 94553. (415) 372-2337.

    Housing rehabilitation loans up to $20,000 carry 3% to 10% interest.

54. Concord/Walnut Creek Community Development, 1950 Parkside Drive, Concord, Calif. 94519. (415) 671-3364.

    Interest rate of 10.8% with 4.5 points.

55. Marin County Housing Authority, PO Box 4282, San Rafael, Calif. 94913. (415) 472-3602.

    Four programs available: Participating townhouse and condominium developments offer 9.9% fixed-rate loans with 5% down, under the First-Time Homebuyers Mortgage Program. Also, for a $12 annual fee, the Below Market Rate program sends information throughout the year on low-cost condominiums that occasionally become available. Buyers are selected by lottery. Their rehab program offers property improvement loans up to $15,000 with interest from 4% to 10%. Finally, the DUO program assists homeowners in adding second living units to their property.

56. San Francisco Mayor's Office in Housing and Economic Development, 100 Larkin Street, San Francisco, Calif. 94102. (415) 558-2881.

    Ask for fact sheet on single-family mortgage

revenue bonds. Interest of 7.5% or 9.8% with 5% down. Qualifying ratio of 33%/38%. These assumable loans are available through participating developers.

57. San Francisco Redevelopment Agency, 939 Ellis, San Francisco, Calif. 94109. (415) 771-8800.

The Affordable Condominium Program keeps monthly housing costs down in exchange for part of the profit upon selling. The Expandable Homes Program assists in the purchase of special small, but expandable, homes.

58. San Mateo County Housing and Community Development, County Government Center, Redwood City, Calif. 94063. (415) 363-4412.

Rehabilitation loans from 3% to 6% available in various target areas. Maximum loan is $35,000.

59. Menlo Park Department of Redevelopment, 701 Laurel Street, Menlo Park, Calif. 94025. (415) 858-3414.

In target areas, rehab loans up to $25,000 are available with interest rates from 3% to 12%.

60. San Mateo City Community Development Department, 330 West 20th Avenue, San Mateo, Calif. 94403-1388. (415) 377-3390.

Meadow Court condominium development is earmarked for first-time buyers.

61. Santa Clara County Community Development Department, 70 West Hedding Street, San Jose, Calif. 95110. (408) 299-4711.

The 1985 Mortgage Revenue Bond carries interest of 9.25% with 5% down, and is available from certain developers. Qualifying ratio is 33%/38%.

62. Palo Alto Housing Improvement Program, 250 Hamilton Avenue, Palo Alto, Calif. 94301. (415) 329-2513.

For low-income households, loans up to $25,000 at 5% interest are available for home rehabilitation. Also, the Energy Services Department offers "Residential Conservation Loans" up to $1,000 to insulate your home.

63. San Jose Department of Neighborhood Preservation, 4 N. Second Street, Suite 950, San Jose, Calif. 95113. (408) 277-4747.

Send a legal size, self-addressed, stamped envelope for a list of developers participating in the 1985 Mortgage Revenue Bond Program. Qualifying ratios are 33%/38% on these 9-7/8% fixed-rate loans.

64. San Jose Redevelopment Department, 101 Park Center Plaza, Suite 1100, San Jose, Calif. 95113. (408) 277-5823.

Provides deferred second mortgage, typically seven years at 4% interest. Ask for a list of developers participating in the "20% Housing Program."

65. Sunnyvale Housing Division, 456 West Olive Avenue, PO Box 60607, Sunnyvale, Calif. 94088. (415) 730-7250.

Fully amortized 15-year loans available for housing rehabilitation. Loan limit of $20,000 on these 4% or 7% fixed-rate loans.

Information on Buyer's Brokers:

66. Buyer's Brokerage. See reference #3.
67. National Association of Real Estate Buyer's Brokers, 1754 Terrace Drive, Belmont, Calif. 94002. (415) 591-6807.

Call for names of buyer's brokers in your area.

68. Buyer's Brokers Registry, Who's Who in Creative Real Estate, PO Box 23275, Ventura, Calif. 93002. (805) 643-2337.

The national directory costs $25.00, but for $5.00, you may receive the names of three buyer's brokers in your area. All brokers they recommend meet their strict qualifying guidelines.

Cooperative Housing:

69. Alternatives Center, 2375 Shattuck Avenue, Berkeley, Calif. 94704. (415) 644- 8336.

    Assists in all phases of developing limited-equity cooperatives.

70. Community Economics, 1904 Franklin Street, Suite 900, Oakland, Calif. 94612. (415) 832-8300.

    Assists community and tenant groups in all phases of arranging low to medium-income group housing. Order "Introduction to Cooperative Conversions." $6.00 + tax.

71. Innovative Housing, 69 Greenbrae Boardwalk, San Rafael, Calif. 94904. (415) 461-4201.

    Shared housing program that includes leasing, purchasing and developing cooperative communities.

72. Innovative Community Housing, 1642 Arch Street, Berkeley, Calif. 94709. (415) 548-6608.

    Workshops and consultations on designing and executing a shared living arrangement.

73. Resources for Community Development, 2375 Shattuck Avenue, Berkeley, Calif. 94704. (415) 841-4410.

    Assists in the creation of limited-equity co-ops and low-income housing in Berkeley.

74. Savings Associations Mortgage Company, 1333 Lawrence Expressway, Suite 330, Santa Clara, Calif. 95051. (408) 985-8110.

    Finances "socially oriented" housing projects. Majority of the projects are rentals, but have financed several limited-equity co-ops.

Mortgage Survey Sources:

75. Local Papers, See Figure 11.
76. Real/Net, 1410 Danzig Plaza, Suite 102, Concord, Calif. 94520. (415) 827-3553.

    An information service providing mortgage tables to most Bay Area newspapers. For

$14.95 you may receive a list of nearly 160 Bay Area lenders and their current rates. Specifies which lenders lock in their rates. Also, the same method of APR calculation is applied to all lenders, so APR has some significance from Real/Net.

77. HSH Associates, Ten Mead Avenue, Riverdale, N.J. 07457. (800) 522-8292.
For $29 they send their Home Buyer's Kit, which includes a guide to choosing mortgages and four weekly "Residential Mortgage Updates," each of which lists the weekly rates for over 60 California lenders. All but a dozen of the lenders are in Southern California. Call for free brochure.

78. Realtors, local agencies.
Realtors subscribe to additional mortgage survey services. These additional services are not listed here because either they are only available to realtors, or the survey company is also a mortgage broker, and therefore the survey is not very comprehensive.

Housing Counseling Centers:

These agencies are partly funded by HUD. They provide free home-purchase guidance to low and medium-income buyers. A valuable resource.

79. ECHO Housing Assistance Center, 770 A Street, Room 402, Hayward, Calif. 94541. (415) 581-9380.
80. Housing Service Center, 110 East Gish Road, San Jose, Calif. 95112. (408) 287-2464.
81. Oakland Office of Community Development, 1417 Clay Street, Oakland, Calif. 94612. (415) 273-3056.
82. Pacific Community Services, PO Box 1397, 510 Railroad Avenu, Pittsburg, Calif. 94565. (415) 439-1056.
83. Richmond Housing Department, 330 25th Street, Richmond, Calif. 94804. (415) 620-6827.

References and Resources

Low-Income Housing Advocates:

84. National Low-Income Housing Coalition, 1012 14th Street, N.W., Suite 1006, Washington, DC. 20005. (202) 662-1530.
    National advocacy group for low-income housing. No programs or literature for first-time home buyers, yet a group deserving of your membership support.
85. Progressive Housing Alliance, 1900 K Street, Sacramento, CA 95814. (916) 446-7904.
    A state version of the National Low Income Housing Coalition.

Miscellaneous:

86. American Home Shield, 7950 Dublin Blvd. #300, Dublin, Calif. 94568. (415) 828-6710.
    Provides one-year home warranties covering malfunctions due to normal wear and tear in wiring, plumbing, built-in appliances, water heater, and furnace. Call for brochure.
87. Bay Guardian, 2700 19th Street, San Francisco, Calif. 94110. (415) 824-7660.
    In February or March they publish two "Superlists": "Free Tax Assistance in San Francisco" and "Free Tax Assistance in the East Bay." Superlists may be mail ordered for $1.50 each.
88. California Apartment Association, 1107 Ninth Street, Suite 1010, Sacramento, Calif. 95814-3607. (916) 447-7881
    Call for information on property owners associations near you.
89. California Department of Real Estate, 185 Berry, Rm. 5816, San Francisco, Calif. 94107. (415) 557-3953.
    Phone them to determine whether disciplinary action has ever been taken against a particular agent, or to file a complaint against an agent.

90. Coldwell Banker, 7950 Dublin Blvd. Suite 100, Dublin, Calif. 94568. (415) 833-6600.
    For those considering a move into or out of the Bay Area, Coldwell Banker has "relocation guides" that give information on home prices, local culture, weather, and much more for various locales nationwide.

91. Ecumenical Association for Housing, 1510 Fifth Avenue, San Rafael, Calif. (415) 453-4887.
    Community organization involved in many housing projects. Ask for current list of projects and programs.

92. Fannie Mae Answer Desk, PO Box 24019, Los Angeles, Calif. 90042. (213) 209-6125 or (213) 209-6463.
    Confused by the rules and regulations of the Federal National Mortgage Association? The Answer Desk staff provides helpful assistance. Also, request their free brochures "A New ARM for Today's Home Buyer" and "How a 15-Year Mortgage Can Help You Save For the Future."

93. Fannie Mae Properties, PO Box 13165, Baltimore, Maryland 21203. (800) 553-4636.
    To receive information on repossessed homes that the Federal National Mortgage Association has for sale, phone or write to them indicating your state and county.

94. Home Owners Warranty Corp., 500 Grapevine Highway, Suite 300, Hurst, TX. 76054. (800) 433-7657
    Ask for the pamphlet "Home Buyer's Guide to HOW."

95. Property Inspection Service, 1741 Saratoga Avenue, Suite 106, San Jose, Calif. 95129. (415)446-9400.
    Request their free checklist booklet "Don't Forget the Most Important Piece."

96. San Francisco <u>Examiner</u>
    Every Wednesday the "Neighborhood" section
    lists weekly crime reports, home sales, fire
    calls, and much more for San Francisco and
    the East Bay.
97. TRW Credit Reports, PO Box 8179, Foster City,
    Calif. 94404. (415) 571-6085.
    Most lenders use TRW's credit reports when
    determining a borrower's credit rating. If,
    within the past 30 days, you have been refused
    credit as a result of the TRW report, you may
    receive your credit report for free. Other-
    wise, the report costs $8 through the mail.
98. US Mortgage Shopper, PO Box 2184, Westport,
    Conn. 06880. (203) 454-2520.
    Send $1.50 to receive their informative eight-
    page booklet, "Tips on Buying a Mortgage" and
    a handy mortgage comparison form. If you
    mail in the form, with $49.95, they perform a
    comparative analysis of four loans you are
    considering.
99. First-Time Home Buyers Consulting Service, 6116
    Merced Avenue, Box 211, Oakland, Calif. 94611.
    (415) 486-1310.
    The author's consulting firm. Both one-on-one
    consulting and seminars are available. Call
    for details.

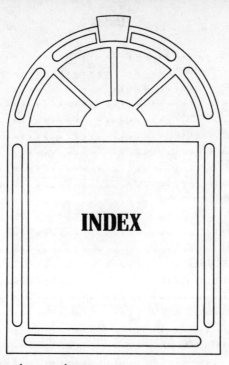

INDEX

Index

ORDER FORM

The Window of Affordability

1 to 9 copies: _____ at $5.95 each   _____

10 or more copies: _____ at $4.00 each_____

California residents add 6% sales tax: _____

Shipping: Add $1.00 for the first book,
and $.25 for each additional book _____

Total: $_____

Name_____

Address_____

City_____St.____Zip_____

Please make check payable to
STRATOSPHERE PUBLISHING.

Mail to:
Stratosphere Publishing
6116 Merced Avenue
Box 211
Oakland, Calif. 94611

Allow three weeks for delivery.